W9-AHG-862

KING
LEAR

Caitlyn Paley

New York

Published in 2016 by Cavendish Square Publishing, LLC
243 5th Avenue, Suite 136, New York, NY 10016

Copyright © 2016 by Cavendish Square Publishing, LLC

First Edition

No part of this publication may be reproduced, stored in a retrieval system, or transmitted in any form or by any means—
electronic, mechanical, photocopying, recording, or otherwise—without the prior permission of the copyright owner. Request
for permission should be addressed to Permissions, Cavendish Square Publishing, 243 5th Avenue, Suite 136, New York, NY
10016. Tel (877) 980-4450; fax (877) 980-4454.

Website: cavendishsq.com

This publication represents the opinions and views of the author based on his or her personal experience, knowledge, and
research. The information in this book serves as a general guide only. The author and publisher have used their best efforts in
preparing this book and disclaim liability rising directly or indirectly from the use and application of this book.

CPSIA Compliance Information: Batch #CW16CSQ

All websites were available and accurate when this book was sent to press.

Cataloging-in-Publication Data

Paley, Caitlyn.
King Lear / by Caitlyn Paley.
p. cm. — (Reading Shakespeare today)
Includes index.
ISBN 978-1-5026-1047-8 (hardcover) ISBN 978-1-5026-1048-5 (e-book)
1. Shakespeare, William, — 1564-1616. — King Lear — Juvenile literature.
2. Shakespeare, William, 1564 -1616 — Criticism and interpretation — Juvenile literature. I. Paley, Caitlyn. II. Title.
PR2819.P35 2016
822.3'3—d23

Editorial Director: David McNamara
Editor: Andrew Coddington
Copy Editor: Rebecca Rohan
Art Director: Jeffrey Talbot
Designer: Stephanie Flecha
Senior Production Manager: Jennifer Ryder-Talbot
Production Editor: Renni Johnson
Photo Research: J8 Media

The photographs in this book are used by permission and through the courtesy of:
Photoshot/Hulton Archive/Getty Images, cover; Shutterstock, front and back covers and through out the book; Unknown,
possibly John Taylor of the Painter-Stainers' Company [1] (Official gallery link) Public Domain, via Wikimedia Commons, 5;
Estate of Emil Bieber/Klaus Niermann/Getty Images, 9; Screengrab of William Shakespeare Twitter page, 11; Culture Club/
Getty Images, 12; Unknown, Public Domain, via Wikimedia Commons, 13; Splash News/Newscom, 15; Heinz-Peter Bader/
REUTERS/Newscom, 19; By Brinkhoff-Moegenburg, professional photographers from Lüneburg. [CC BY-SA 3.0 (http://
creativecommons.org/licenses/by-sa/3.0)], via Wikimedia Commons, 23; Heinz-Peter Bader/Reuters/Newscom, 28; Ray Tang/
REX/Newscom, 31; Christie's Images Ltd./Superstock, 36; King Lear (engraving), English School, (19th century)/Private
Collection/Look and Learn/Bridgeman Images, 39; Tony Larkin/REX/Newscom, 43; Johan Persson/ArenaPal/The Image
Works, 49; Belinsky Yuri Itar-Tass Photos/Newscom, 51; Kurov Alexander Itar-Tass Photos/Newscom, 52; Greg Wood/AFP/
Getty Images, 55; William Blake/Public Domain, via Wikimedia Commons, 59; ANNE-CHRISTINE POUJOULAT/AFP/Getty
Images, 62; © 2014 Mya Gosling, 64; Alastair Muir/Rex Features/AP Images, 66; King Lear (engraving), Henry Courtney
Selous/Private Collection/Look and Learn/Bridgeman Images, 75; Tony Larkin/REX/Newscom, 78; Stephanie Methven/WENN/
Newscom, 81; By Anonymous (Galerie dramatique) Public Domain, via Wikimedia Commons, 84; Illustration for the cover of
'Finding Out, Shakespeare's World', published by Purnell and Sons Ltd., London 1964 (gouache on paper), Anne Johnstone &
Janet Johnstone/Private Collection/Bridgeman Images, 89; John Michael Wright/Public Domain, via Wikimedia Commons, 90;
By Jessie Chapman (Own work) [CC BY-SA 4.0 (http://creativecommons.org/licenses/by-sa/4.0)], via Wikimedia Commons, 92.

Printed in the United States of America

CONTENTS

Introduction

SHAKESPEARE AND HIS WORLD

Illiam Shakespeare is, perhaps, the most famous writer of all time. Over hundreds of years, Shakespeare has become a towering figure. His reputation is the stuff of myth. In fact, his fame has led to some important questions. Who was Shakespeare really? What do we know about him for certain? Where does the man end and the legend begin?

Historians believe that William Shakespeare was born to a large family in England in April 1564. His father John was a glove maker and public official who struggled to keep the family out of debt. Otherwise, Shakespeare's childhood is mostly a mystery. The absence of school records, letters, and other primary sources means that scholars can only develop theories about how a small boy from Stratford-upon-Avon grew up to be a prolific writer. He might have attended a local grammar school to receive instruction in Latin and reading. Yet many experts believe that Shakespeare taught himself to read without the benefit of a formal education.

We do know that Shakespeare married Anne Hathaway in 1582. William was eighteen years old; Anne was twenty-six. In the next year and a half, they had three children:

William Shakespeare was born almost five centuries ago, but his plays and poems have stood the test of time.

a daughter named Susanna, followed by twins named Hamnet and Judith. Hamnet died eleven years later, triggering the saddest period of Shakespeare's life. Shortly after starting his family, Shakespeare became involved in the world of theater.

Records indicate that in the 1590s, Shakespeare joined London's foremost acting company, the Lord Chamberlain's Men. It was also in the 1590s that Shakespeare's writing gained notice. Shakespeare's poem *Venus and Adonis* was published in 1593. His next publication was another poem, *The Rape of Lucrece*. Both poems were enormously successful. Shakespeare established himself as one of the strongest poets of the era.

Despite the precise information about Shakespeare's early writing career, scholars remain uncertain about the publication dates of Shakespeare's plays. However, it seems that he was an instant success as a playwright, too. Shakespeare became a partner in the Lord Chamberlain's Men, who performed at the Globe Theatre in the mid-1590s.

Shakespeare is best known for works like *Romeo and Juliet*, *Othello*, *Macbeth*, *The Merchant of Venice*, *Julius Caesar*, and *A Midsummer Night's Dream*. He wrote tragedies, comedies, and historical plays that have stood the test of time.

Today, over four hundred years later, children grow up knowing the basic plots of his plays. No other playwright has achieved this level of enduring fame. More impressive is the way that Shakespeare's work continues to shape our culture. Lines from his thirty-seven plays have even entered our everyday speech. Theater companies around the world perform his works. Movies and television shows continue to adapt his stories in new and exciting ways. And all of this stems from a man who retired before he turned fifty! Shakespeare spent his last years in his hometown of Stratford, where he died in 1616. *Mr. William Shakespeares Comedies, Histories, & Tragedies*, an anthology of his writing, was published seven years later. Often called the First Folio, it contained thirty-six of his plays and is credited with the preservation of Shakespeare's canon.

Chapter One

Shakespeare and *King Lear*

Most scholars have settled on 1605 as the most likely date of *King Lear's* composition, which would place it between *Othello* and *Macbeth*. One of Shakespeare's most complex works, both in structure and in content, *King Lear* is considered one of Shakespeare's greatest masterpieces, rivaled only by *Hamlet*.

The Evolution of the Plot

The story of King Lear did not originate with Shakespeare. In the twelfth century, Geoffrey of Monmouth had placed Lear among the earliest kings of Britain—in the eighth century BCE—in his *Historia Regum Britanniae (The History of the Kings of Britain)*. Leir (as his real name was spelled) was the longest-ruling of all the British kings, having reigned in southwest England for sixty years before dividing his kingdom between his two oldest daughters.

Alex Otto starred in a production of *King Lear* in 1920. The role has been played by many notable actors over the years.

Shakespeare likely derived most of his knowledge of Leir from Raphael Holinshed's *Chronicles of England, Scotlande, and Irelande*, which was first published in 1577. Shakespeare's incorporation of the Gloucester subplot in *King Lear* is only one of the changes he made to the

Friending Shakespeare

IT'S HARD TO imagine what the Bard would think of his presence on social media. Perhaps he'd think it would confirm the idea that "All the world's a stage." Regardless of what Shakespeare would think about Twitter or Facebook, once you start looking, you'll notice him on just about every platform. On Pinterest, Shakespeare pops up on quotation boards. Quotations like "Though she be but little, she is fierce," and "I would challenge you to a battle of wits, but I see you are unarmed," are favorites on the site. Shakespearean insults and embedded videos of performances are on boards all over Pinterest. Many pinners share BuzzFeed quizzes and articles about Shakespeare. BuzzFeed's quizzes assign readers a character from Shakespeare's plays or test readers' knowledge.

On Twitter, users tweet favorite lines, promote local performances, and share links to the latest Shakespeare scholarship. The Royal Shakespeare Company even adapted Romeo and Juliet for Twitter. Accounts like @ShakespeareSays and @Shakespeare not only quote Shakespeare, but also react to pop culture in his persona. These Twitter accounts promote events like "Talk Like Shakespeare Day" (April 23) with the hashtag #TalkLikeShakespeare.

But it is perhaps Facebook where it's most clear that Shakespeare's legacy is alive and well. William Shakespeare's author page on Facebook might be the best way to stay tuned to up-to-the-minute Shakespeare news. The page's timeline highlights innovative performances, projects, and adaptations of Shakespeare's work. There are pictures and biographical information, too.

The page has fostered an active community. It's not unusual to see a post with twelve thousand likes and over one thousand shares. And while it's difficult to quantify Shakespeare's continued popularity, it should be noted that his page has over sixteen million followers.

The Twitter page for William Shakespeare proves the playwright's continued influence, even as technology replaces pen-and-ink books.

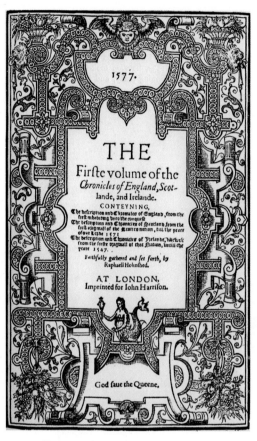

The

Firfte volume of the
Chronicles of England, Scot-
lande, and Irelande.
CONTEYNING,
The defcription and Chronicles of England, from the
firft inhabiting vnto the conqueft
The defcription and Chronicles of Scotland, from the
firft original of the Scottes nation, till the yeare
of our Lorde 1571
The defcription and Chronicles of Yrelande, likewife
from the firfte original of that Ɲation, vntill the
yeare 1547.
Faithfully gathered and fet forth, by
Raphaell Holinfhed.

AT LONDON,
Imprinted for Iohn Harrifon.

God faue the Queene.

Shakespeare's *King Lear* differs from the account
of King Leir in the Holinshed manuscript.

traditional narrative that were significant enough to make it his own. Shakespeare's decision to end the play with the deaths of both Cordelia and Lear was long criticized for departing from the Monmouth and Holinshed versions, in which Leir returned triumphant to the throne, to be succeeded by Cordelia.

Shakespeare's decision to make Lear's insanity central to the plot may have had a contemporary historical parallel in the case of Sir Brian Annesley. Annesley's eldest daughter tried to take control of his estate in 1603 by having him declared insane, and she was supported by her younger sister. Annesley's youngest daughter, Cordell, interceded on behalf of her father.

Shakespeare's audience would have been familiar with the Annesley case, as well as with broader political themes that are reflected in the play. In 1603, as childless Queen

Queen Elizabeth I left no heirs, and the public's concern about succession influenced Shakespeare's *King Lear*.

Elizabeth I approached death, many in England feared that political divisions would destroy the country. Such fears were allayed when James VI of Scotland, next in line to the throne of England, succeeded Elizabeth upon her death and became James I of England.

Chapter Two

The Play's
The Thing

Act I, Scene 1

Overview

In the palace of Lear, king of Britain, the Earl of Kent and the Earl of Gloucester discuss Lear's plan to divide his kingdom and give up his throne. Kent and Gloucester, two of Lear's advisers, agree that in the past Lear had seemed to prefer the Duke of Albany to the Duke of Cornwall. Albany is the husband of Lear's eldest daughter, Goneril; Cornwall, the husband of Lear's second daughter, Regan. Now, however, it appears that Lear may divide his kingdom equally among his three daughters.

Kent asks Gloucester whether the third man in the scene, Edmund, is his son; Gloucester admits that Edmund is his "whoreson"—that is, a bastard, a child conceived and born out of wedlock. Although Gloucester has been reluctant to acknowledge Edmund in the past, he says he is now as pleased with Edmund as he is with his legitimate son, Edgar.

At the beginning of the play, Lear (played here by Sir Ian McKellen) prepares to give up the crown and divide his kingdom among his three daughters.

A trumpet announces the arrival of Lear, who is followed by Albany, Cornwall, and Lear's three daughters. Lear explains the purpose of his plan: by dividing Britain into three parts and giving up his crown while he is still alive, Lear hopes to avoid war between his daughters' husbands after his death. How Britain will be divided, however, depends on a contest that Lear has devised. Each daughter must explain why she loves him more than her sisters do.

Lear's eldest daughter, Goneril, declares that she loves Lear as much as a child has ever loved a father. While Lear announces Goneril's portion of the kingdom, his youngest daughter, Cordelia, tells the audience that she will remain quiet when it is her turn.

Lear's middle daughter, Regan, tells her father that she not only loves him as much as Goneril does, but more, because Regan is only happy when she is with Lear. In return, Lear grants Regan a portion of Britain equal to that which he gave to Goneril. In an aside, Cordelia tells the audience that her love for Lear is so great that she cannot put it into words.

Turning to his youngest daughter, Lear does not conceal that he favors Cordelia above her sisters. He offers Cordelia the best third of his kingdom if she will simply declare her love for him as her sisters did. Cordelia tells her father that she will say nothing. Lear, stunned, gives Cordelia a second and then a third chance to speak. Instead, Cordelia tells Lear that she simply loves him as a daughter should. Her answer enrages Lear, who swears by the gods that he disowns Cordelia.

Kent tries to convince Lear that he has misunderstood: Cordelia truly loves Lear. This only makes Lear angrier, and the king banishes Kent from Britain on pain of death. As Kent leaves, he asks the gods to protect Cordelia and urges Regan and Goneril to turn their words of love toward Lear into action. Meanwhile, Lear divides Cordelia's third of the kingdom between Albany and Cornwall and divides his crown—his royal authority—between them. Lear makes only one condition: he will spend alternate months with Goneril and Regan, and the daughters will house and feed his one hundred knights.

Gloucester brings the King of France and the Duke of Burgundy—the two rivals for Cordelia's hand in marriage—into the hall. When Burgundy hears that he will not get a third of the kingdom, he loses interest in Cordelia. Lear tries to convince the King of France to cast Cordelia aside as well, but Cordelia explains her actions to the French king, who takes her as his queen. Saying good-bye to her sisters, Cordelia urges them to treat their father well and predicts that time will tell which of the three sisters loves Lear the most.

The scene ends with Goneril and Regan discussing Lear's impetuous actions toward both Cordelia and Kent, which they blame on the king's age as well as on his rashness. Goneril and Regan resolve to undermine what remains of Lear's authority.

Analysis

In this opening scene, Shakespeare sets up the action, plot, and subplots of the play. Lear, through his division of his kingdom and his disavowal of Cordelia, places himself at the mercy of Goneril and Regan and their husbands. Hoping to avoid strife after his death, Lear has unwittingly created conditions that threaten to destroy Britain. Meanwhile, Gloucester, by drawing his illegitimate son, Edmund, to himself, sets in motion the events that will lead to the earl's own downfall.

Act I, Scene 2

Overview

The action shifts to Gloucester's castle. In a short speech, Edmund contrasts custom, which has branded him illegitimate, with nature. He declares himself physically and mentally at least the equal of his half brother, Edgar, Gloucester's legitimate son. Edmund has decided to turn the tables on his half brother by attempting to convince Gloucester to disown Edgar so that Edmund will inherit Gloucester's land.

As Gloucester enters, Edmund makes a show of hiding a letter. Gloucester notices and asks about it. Edmund pretends that he does not want to show the letter to Gloucester, which makes the earl all the more eager to see it. Edmund declares that the letter is from Edgar and pretends to find its contents disturbing. Feigning reluctance, Edmund hands the letter over to Gloucester. The letter suggests that Edmund should join Edgar in a plot against Gloucester: rather than grow old while waiting for their father to die, the two half brothers will dispose of Gloucester and divide his wealth between them.

Gloucester is upset that Edgar would betray him, and Edmund pretends to be surprised as well. Edmund says he cannot be certain that the letter is from Edgar, since it was supposedly placed in Edmund's study. Still, Edmund tells Gloucester that he has often heard Edgar say that fathers should hand over their wealth to sons when the sons come of age.

Gloucester declares that eclipses of the sun and moon are responsible for recent strange events: Lear's division of the kingdom, the banishment of Kent and Cordelia,

Edmund (Michael Rotschopf) stokes Gloucester's (Martin Reinke) curiosity about the letter that Edmund, in fact, has written as part of his plan to gain power.

and Edgar's seeming betrayal. Yet after Gloucester leaves, Edmund denounces his father's view of fate, regarding it as an evasion of responsibility for one's actions. Edmund declares that he would be the same man if he had been conceived under completely different stars.

As Edgar enters, however, Edmund sighs "like Tom o' Bedlam" and speaks as Gloucester did, pretending to be worried about the effects of the eclipses. Edmund then changes the subject and asks Edgar when he last saw Gloucester. Edmund tells Edgar that Gloucester is upset with Edgar, either because Edgar offended him somehow, or someone has told the earl something untrue concerning Edgar.

Edmund urges Edgar to stay in his rooms until Gloucester calms down. Edmund also advises Edgar to carry a weapon if he must go out. As Edgar leaves, Edmund marvels at Gloucester's gullibility and Edgar's honesty, both of which will make Edmund's plan to usurp Edgar much easier.

Analysis

Gloucester's acknowledgment of Edmund has given him what he needs to usurp Edgar and to gain control of Gloucester's wealth and lands. Edmund has cleverly constructed a plan to make it appear as if Edgar wishes to do what Edmund himself intends. Like Goneril and Regan do with Lear, Edmund flatters his father while acting against him.

The Gloucester-Edmund-Edgar subplot mirrors the main plot of the play. Shakespeare has introduced a conflict between Gloucester's view of the gods, nature, and fate and Edmund's belief that men make their own destinies. Edmund mocks Gloucester's beliefs, but he is willing to use those beliefs to advance his own cause. Edmund also takes advantage of Edgar's honesty to convince his half brother that his lies are the truth. Edmund uses "Tom o' Bedlam" to refer to his mimicking of Gloucester's behavior. In Shakespeare's day, "Tom o' Bedlam" was a generic name given to insane beggars who roamed the countryside.

Act I, Scene 3

Overview

At Albany's palace, Goneril enters with her steward Oswald. Lear no longer has a place of his own, so he and his one hundred knights have been staying with Goneril. Oswald says that Lear has struck him for scolding his Fool. Goneril sees this as evidence that she and Regan were right: Lear is out of control. Moreover, Lear's knights are causing problems, which Goneril plans to resolve by refusing to speak to her father in the hope that he will decide to stay with Regan instead. Goneril orders Oswald to make sure that he and his fellow servants do not go out of their way to please Lear or his knights. Goneril will write a letter advising Regan to treat Lear the same way.

Analysis

Lear has given up all his authority but has retained the title of king, and his one hundred knights are a symbol of that title. However, Goneril decides to treat Lear in a way that does not respect him either as the king or as her father: Goneril will ignore him and will urge Regan to do the same. The actions of Goneril and Regan are proving that their words of love to Lear were false.

Act I, Scene 4

Overview

After Goneril and Oswald leave, Kent enters Albany's palace. Although Lear banished him from Britain on pain of death, Kent still desires to serve him. To do so, however, Kent must appear in disguise.

Lear returns from hunting. Noticing the disguised Kent, Lear asks him who he is and what he wants. Kent answers that he is simply what Lear sees: a trustworthy man. Kent pledges to serve Lear, pretending not to know that Lear is the king of Britain and claiming it is Lear's air of authority that makes him want to serve the old man. Lear agrees to take the disguised Kent into his service, so long as he enjoys Kent's company over dinner.

Catching sight of Oswald, Lear asks where Goneril is. When the steward quickly exits without answering, Lear sends a knight to bring him back. The knight informs Lear that Oswald, who refuses to return, has said that Goneril is not well. Goneril, Albany, and all of their servants, the knight says, have not been treating Lear with the respect he deserves, and the king admits that he has noticed this, too.

Oswald returns, and Lear demands that the steward tell him who he—Lear—is. Oswald responds that Lear is Goneril's father, an answer that enrages the king, who strikes the steward. Kent trips Oswald. Pleased with Kent's action, Lear decides that he can stay in his service.

Hearing this as he enters, the Fool offers his coxcomb (his fool's cap) to Kent. One would have to be a fool to serve Lear, the Fool says, because Lear has fallen out of favor and has made mistakes concerning all three of his

The Fool (Erwin Leder) often wears outlandish costumes in productions of the play. His over-the-top appearance contradicts his wisdom.

daughters. The Fool tells Lear that it was doubly foolish to give up his living—that is, his wealth—to Goneril and Regan. Lear, the Fool says, was born a fool. His authority lay in his crown, not in his intellect. Lear, the Fool points out, has "madest thy daughters thy mother"—that is, given Goneril and Regan authority over him.

As Goneril enters, Lear asks her why she is frowning. Goneril replies that the actions of his knights and attendants, and even of Lear himself, are the cause. Lear is astonished. Goneril's treatment of him shows a lack of respect. The Fool tells Lear why: Lear is but a shadow of his former self.

Goneril insists that Lear reduce the number of his knights. Lear replies by calling her a bastard and declaring his intention to stay with Regan instead. Albany arrives and tries to intervene, telling Lear that he knows nothing of Goneril's plan. Lear begins to regret his treatment of Cordelia now that Goneril's profession of love is not reflected in her actions.

Lear calls upon a nameless goddess and Nature to curse Goneril and make her unable to bear children. Should Goneril have a child, Lear asks that the child be to Goneril what she has been to Lear: a "thankless child" and a "torment."

Lear exits, but quickly returns, having learned the extent of the reduction in his entourage that Goneril wants him to make: one hundred to fifty within two weeks. Lear decides he will go stay with Regan. In Regan's household, Lear declares, he will recover his former authority.

After Lear, Kent, and Lear's attendants leave, Goneril reveals her fear to Albany: it was not safe to let Lear keep a hundred knights, because he would then be able to order her and Albany around. Albany tells Goneril that her fears may be unfounded. Goneril orders Oswald to deliver to Regan the letter explaining her plan and tells him to add reasons of his own to make the letter even more forceful. As Oswald leaves, Goneril chides Albany for his lack of wisdom, yet he tells his wife that she may have made matters worse.

Analysis

Kent's loyalty to Lear is greater than his fear of death. Unlike Goneril and Regan, Kent shows his love to Lear through his actions. The Fool is loyal to Lear in his own way. Even when Lear gets angry at the Fool for telling the truth, the Fool continues to point out that Lear is responsible for his own situation. Daughters should not have authority over their fathers, yet Lear has changed places with Goneril and Regan. Having now renounced both Cordelia and Goneril, Lear is leaving himself at the mercy of his second daughter, Regan.

Act I, Scene 5

Overview

Lear, Kent, and the Fool stand in front of Albany's palace, preparing to depart for Regan's residence. Lear gives a letter to Kent to deliver to Regan in advance of his arrival. As Kent leaves, the Fool tells Lear that Goneril and Regan may seem different on the surface, but that the two daughters are the same. While not mentioning Cordelia by name, Lear says that he "did her wrong." The Fool also says that Lear's mistake goes further: by dividing his kingdom between Goneril and Regan, Lear is like a snail who has given up his shell. As he and the Fool depart, Lear fears that he is losing his sanity and begs heaven that this is not the case.

This scene is short but important. The Fool continues to speak the truth to Lear: the king has gone against the natural order by dividing his kingdom. Goneril's actions are to be expected because she no longer has a reason to respect Lear. Regan, the Fool predicts correctly, will act the same way. While wisdom is supposed to come with age, Lear has not gained it. The destruction in the natural order that Lear has started will be reflected in the destruction of his own nature as he descends into madness.

Act II, Scene 1

Overview

The action shifts to Gloucester's castle, where a member of Gloucester's court tells Edmund that Cornwall and Regan will soon arrive. The courtier does not know the reason for Cornwall's visit, but he tells Edmund that there are rumors of a coming war between Cornwall and Albany. As the courtier leaves, Edmund realizes that he can use Cornwall's arrival to advance his own plan against Edgar.

Edmund calls Edgar onto the scene. Edmund urges his half brother to leave before Cornwall arrives, claiming there are rumors that Edgar has spoken out against Cornwall. Hearing Gloucester coming, Edmund draws his sword and convinces his half brother to do likewise. Edmund calls out to Gloucester and his servants as he sends Edgar away.

Before Gloucester arrives, Edmund cuts his own arm, drawing blood. Stalling for time to let Edgar get away, Edmund tells Gloucester that he found Edgar "conjuring the moon"—that is, casting spells to advance Edgar's supposed plot to murder Gloucester and inherit his land and wealth. Edmund also tells Gloucester that Edgar attacked him when he refused to take part in Edgar's plot.

Gloucester plans to convince Cornwall to close Britain's ports so that Edgar cannot leave the island. A reward will be offered for Edgar's capture, and anyone who hides him will be put to death.

Edmund tells Gloucester that Edgar had claimed that no one would believe Edmund because he is a bastard. Gloucester responds that he will do what it takes to make Edmund the legitimate heir to his land.

Cornwall and Regan arrive, and both allude to rumors of Edgar's plot against Gloucester. Regan notes that Edgar is Lear's godson and, having received Goneril's letter, suggests that Edgar may have come to the plot by associating with Lear's "riotous knights"—a suggestion Edmund quickly supports. Cornwall and Gloucester praise Edmund for his supposed attempt to capture Edgar, and Cornwall takes Edmund into his service. Regan announces that she has received letters from both Lear and Goneril, and she and Cornwall have come to Gloucester to seek his advice on how to proceed.

Analysis

Just as Lear's subversion of the natural order has begun to have its effects, Edmund's attempt to usurp both Edgar and Gloucester is beginning to bear fruit. Edmund puts the words of his own plot into Edgar's mouth, knowing that he has turned Gloucester against Edgar already. The strategy pays off: Gloucester seals his own fate by disowning Edgar, who has been loyal, and embracing Edmund, whose words of loyalty cover the disloyalty of his action.

Act II, Scene 2

Kent and Oswald arrive in front of Gloucester's castle. While both men have come from Albany's palace, they have traveled separately, and Oswald does not immediately recognize Kent. When Oswald asks Kent where he can put his horse, Kent tells him to put the horse in the swamp.

The men begin to argue, and when Oswald complains that Kent should not speak this way to a stranger, Kent reveals that he was the man who tripped Oswald after Lear struck him. Kent orders Oswald to draw his sword so that

Cornwall and Regan disrespect Lear by placing Kent (Branko Samarovski) in the stocks like a common criminal.

they can fight. When Oswald instead cries for help, Kent beats him with the flat of his sword.

Oswald's cries attract Edmund, Gloucester, Cornwall, and Regan. With sword drawn, Edmund separates Kent and Oswald. Gloucester and Cornwall demand an explanation for the fight, while Regan notes that Kent and Oswald were sent by Lear and Goneril, respectively. Oswald tells Cornwall that he cannot speak because he is out of breath, and Kent mocks the steward for his cowardice in refusing to draw his sword.

As Cornwall and Gloucester attempt to find out what caused the fight, Kent says that it was simply natural that he would grow angry at "such a knave" (a dishonest man) as Oswald. When Cornwall, frustrated by Kent's bluntness, says that he and his companions dislike Kent as much as Oswald does, Kent insults all of those assembled. Cornwall then asks Oswald how he offended Kent, and the steward tells the story of Lear striking him and Kent tripping him.

Cornwall orders that Kent be put in the stocks until noon, despite Kent's objection that placing him in the stocks would show little respect for Lear. Regan goes further, saying that Kent should be kept in the stocks all day and all night. Gloucester intervenes, noting that the stocks normally are only used for common criminals and that Lear will be upset that his messenger was treated in such a way. Cornwall and Regan are unmoved, and Kent is placed in the stocks.

After Edmund, Oswald, Cornwall, and Regan leave, Gloucester tells Kent that he is sorry for what has happened and predicts again that Lear will be angry when he finds him in the stocks. As Gloucester leaves, Kent reads a letter from Cordelia, who has learned of Lear's troubles and promises to come to her father's aid. Confined in the stocks, Kent falls asleep.

Analysis

Kent is punished for his bluntness, that same willingness to speak the truth that led Lear to banish him from Britain in Act I, Scene 1. Kent's bluntness is in defense of Lear.

While Cornwall and Regan have come to seek Gloucester's advice, Gloucester, who had doubted from the beginning the wisdom of Lear's plan to divide the kingdom, is disturbed by the treatment of Kent. Gloucester, like Kent, is still loyal to the king.

Act II, Scene 3

Overview

Edgar has eluded Gloucester's men thus far, but the ports are closed, and people everywhere are on the lookout for him. Edgar decides that the best way to keep from being captured is to take on a disguise: he will become a lunatic beggar, covering himself in dirt and wearing only a cloth about his waist. "Edgar I nothing am," he declares; he will go by the name of Tom.

Analysis

In Act I, Scene 2, Edmund had sighed "like Tom o' Bedlam" when he lied to Edgar. Now Edgar, disguising himself in order to evade capture and possibly even death, becomes a "Bedlam beggar" named Tom. Like Kent, Edgar will bear his exile in disguise and be able to speak his mind because no one will recognize him.

A costume change transforms Edgar (Trystan Gravelle) into Tom o' Bedlam.

Act II, Scene 4

Overview

Lear, the Fool, and a Gentleman arrive in front of Gloucester's castle. Lear finds it strange that Regan and Cornwall did not send Kent back to him after he delivered Lear's letter to them. Kent, who has spent the night in the stocks, calls out to Lear. Lear demands to know who would show so little respect for his messenger. When Kent tells Lear that Cornwall and Regan have ordered him placed in the stocks, Lear cannot believe it. He insists that Kent must have done something to deserve the punishment, but Kent recounts the events, ending with his confrontation with Oswald.

The Fool has an explanation for Regan's desire to punish Lear's messenger: when fathers are wealthy and bestow goods on their children, their children are kind to their fathers; when fathers are poor, however, their children become "blind"—that is, ungrateful.

Telling the Fool and the Gentleman to stay with Kent, Lear enters the castle to find Regan. Meanwhile, in riddle and rhyme, the Fool answers Kent's question about why Lear's company has greatly decreased: now that Lear has fallen out of favor with his own daughters and cannot pay them, the knights have left him. The Fool, however, says that he will remain loyal.

Lear returns with Gloucester, furious that Regan and Cornwall have refused to speak with him. Lear looks at Kent and declares that the act of placing his messenger in the stocks proves that Regan and Cornwall are deliberately ignoring him. Lear tells Gloucester that he himself will fetch Regan and Cornwall if they do not come to him. Gloucester goes to relay this message and shortly thereafter returns with Regan and Cornwall.

As Cornwall and Regan greet Lear, Kent is set free. As Lear relates Goneril's treatment of him, Regan rises to her sister's defense, saying that Goneril did the right thing in putting restrictions on Lear's knights. Regan declares that Lear is in need of someone to rule him and suggests that he return to Goneril and ask her to forgive him. Lear says that such an action would make him no better than a beggar and vows never to return to Goneril. Lear curses Goneril, and Regan replies that he will do the same to Regan when he is upset with her. Lear denies this, saying that Regan would never do the things that Goneril has done because Regan remembers her duty.

As if immediately doubting his own words, Lear asks who put Kent in the stocks.

Lear has begun to suspect that Regan is more like Goneril than he had thought. Goneril arrives and Regan takes her sister's hand, confirming Lear's fears. Lear asks one last time who put Kent into the stocks, and Cornwall admits that the order was his.

Regan urges Lear to dismiss half of his knights and to return to Goneril for the rest of the month before coming to live with her, but Lear refuses. Lear says that he would sooner be homeless, or throw himself on the mercy of the King of France, or even be a slave to Oswald. Goneril tells Lear that the choice is his.

Lear resigns himself to Goneril's treatment of him. Goneril is still his daughter, Lear says, and one day she will come to her senses. In the meantime, he and his one hundred knights will stay with Regan. Not so fast, Regan replies. Lear can return to Goneril and keep fifty knights, but if Lear insists on coming to live with Regan, she will allow him to have only twenty-five. Lear decides that Goneril does not seem so bad after all; he will go with her and keep fifty of his knights. Goneril, however, has changed her mind. Both daughters now say that Lear needs no knights; their own servants should be enough for him. Lear blames the gods for the ingratitude of his daughters and asks them to grant him anger that will overwhelm his sympathy. He vows vengeance on Goneril and Regan and declares that he will go mad.

As a storm arises, Lear, Gloucester, Kent, and the Fool depart. Regan and Goneril renew their resolve not to take Lear in if he brings any knights. Gloucester returns to tell them that Lear is exceedingly angry and has decided to leave. Gloucester is worried because the landscape is forbidding and the storm is coming on; however, Regan and Cornwall urge Gloucester to let Lear go and to shut the doors of the castle.

Analysis

The full fruits of Lear's decision to divide his kingdom and give up his authority are on display. Goneril and Regan have no further use for their father. Rather than bidding for his affection by trying to trump each other by letting Lear keep more of his knights, they bid each other down until both say that Lear should have no knights or other servants.

The storm is a reflection in nature of the disorder in the kingdom of Britain. Lear fears that he is losing his sanity, and his action confirms that fear: he decides to leave the safety of Gloucester's castle and venture out into the storm. Goneril and Regan show their complete lack of affection for their father by telling Gloucester to shut the doors of the castle, leaving Lear stranded in the tempest.

Act III, Scene 1

Overview

As the storm rages, Kent encounters the Gentleman who had earlier accompanied Lear to Gloucester's castle. Both are looking for Lear on the heath, an area of open land with only small bushes and no shelter from the storm. The Gentleman tells Kent that Lear is alone with the Fool and seems to be losing his sanity, tearing at his hair and calling for the destruction of Britain.

Kent reveals to the Gentleman that Albany and Cornwall are plotting against each other. Through spies in the households of Albany and Cornwall, the King of France knows of this division and has decided to move on Britain. Kent sends the Gentleman to the port of Dover with instructions to let France know of Lear's plight. While Kent remains in disguise, he gives the Gentleman a ring and tells him that Cordelia will recognize it and thus know who sent him to her. As the Gentleman leaves, Kent resumes his search for Lear.

Analysis

The storm reflects both the state of Lear's mind and the state of the kingdom of Britain. Lear is calling on nature to destroy the island, but his own actions have set into motion the events that are tearing Britain apart. While Kent knows that the King of France acts on behalf of Cordelia (and thus will act on behalf of Lear), France is still a foreign power whose victory would mean Britain's defeat.

Act III, Scene 2

Overview

Meanwhile, on another part of the heath, Lear and the Fool are caught in the storm. Lear is urging nature to destroy the world. The Fool suggests that Lear should return to Regan and Goneril and spend the night in safety.

Kent finds Lear and the Fool. Kent declares that the storm is the worst he has ever seen and that men cannot stand such weather either physically or mentally. Lear sees the storm as the work of the gods, who are uncovering the crimes of men; he says, however, that he is "More sinned against than sinning."

The Fool and Lear, whose head is bare, endure the tempest.

Kent notes that Lear's head is bare and directs him to a hovel—a small structure that will at least provide some protection against the elements. Kent will go seek help at a house nearby. As Lear and Kent leave the stage, the Fool offers a "prophecy" in rhyme: when men act as they should in England, the country will be a very different place.

Analysis

On one hand, Lear is right that he is "More sinned against than sinning." Goneril and Regan have not treated Lear with the respect that he is due as their father. On the other hand, as the Fool has repeatedly made clear, Lear's sufferings are of his own making. Lear's head is bare not only because it is exposed to the elements, but because he has given up his crown.

Act III, Scene 3

Overview

Back at Gloucester's castle, Gloucester tells Edmund that Lear is being treated unnaturally by Goneril, Regan, and their husbands. When Gloucester spoke on Lear's behalf, Regan and Goneril turned on him. But, Gloucester says, all will be made right soon. Albany and Cornwall are divided, and he himself has received a letter indicating that forces have already landed in Britain that will take Lear's side. Gloucester, too, will support Lear, even if it costs him his life, and he asks Edmund to speak with Cornwall so that Cornwall will not suspect Gloucester of favoring Lear.

When Gloucester leaves, Edmund tells the audience that he will find the letter, take it to Cornwall, and let him know that Gloucester supports Lear. Gloucester will lose his land and wealth, and Edmund, whom Cornwall has already taken into his service, will receive it all.

Analysis

Gloucester's story has reached its turning point. He assumes that Edmund shares his loyalty to Lear—an assumption that will cost Gloucester greatly. Edmund is loyal only to himself; he will use Gloucester's loyalty to Lear to usurp his father, just as he earlier usurped his half brother, Edgar.

Act III, Scene 4

Overview

Back on the heath, Lear, Kent, and the Fool arrive at the hovel. Kent tries to convince Lear to enter, but he wants to stay out in the storm. The elements, Lear says, are a lesser ill than what he has suffered at the hands of Regan and Goneril.

As Lear sends the Fool into the hovel, he reflects that, as king, he thought little about his less-fortunate subjects who had no shelter against the weather on nights such as this. Lear's reflection is interrupted by a voice from within the hovel. It is Edgar, disguised as Tom o' Bedlam.

Kent orders Edgar to come out. Edgar pretends to be tormented by a demon, and Lear asks him whether he has been driven to madness by giving all that he owned to his own daughters. Only the ingratitude of daughters, Lear says, could bring a man to Edgar's condition.

As Edgar continues to rant, Lear asks, "Is man no more than this?" As Tom o' Bedlam, Edgar is man in his natural state. His condition is reflected in his clothing; he

Lear refuses to enter the hovel, preferring to experience the elements.

wears only a blanket around his waist. Lear begins to tear off his own clothes just as Gloucester arrives.

Edgar continues to rant in pretend madness, and his father, Gloucester, does not recognize him. Gloucester urges Lear to return with him. Lear, Kent tells Gloucester, is losing his sanity. That is only natural, Gloucester replies, since Lear's "daughters seek his death." Not realizing that he is talking to Kent in disguise, Gloucester praises the earl for his earlier prediction that Lear's banishment of Cordelia would end in tragedy.

Gloucester says that he can understand Lear's madness, because he himself has a son, Edgar, who wishes to kill him. Since Lear insists on speaking to the disguised Edgar as if Edgar were a wise man, Gloucester tells Lear to bring him along as the party finds shelter from the storm.

Analysis

Edgar has decided to pretend not only to be insane but to be tormented by a demon, a decision that will play an important role in his later dealings with Gloucester.

Lear had told his daughters that his knights were to him what a woman's clothes are to her: a symbol of her status. Now Lear tears at his own clothes, which symbolize the difference between himself and the insane beggar, Tom. Lear is not only going insane, he welcomes insanity, because it will relieve him of his sorrow over Goneril and Regan.

Act III, Scene 5

Overview

Back at Gloucester's castle, Edmund has put the final touches on his plan. Cornwall announces that he will have revenge upon Gloucester. Edmund pretends to be torn between his natural bond to his father and his loyalty to Cornwall, but he declares that he will remain loyal to the latter. Cornwall declares that Edmund is now the earl of Gloucester, explaining that Gloucester's concealment of the letter about France's forces proves Gloucester's treachery. Cornwall orders Edmund to find Gloucester. While Edmund has lost his natural father, Cornwall will become a "dearer father" through his trust in Edmund.

Analysis

Edmund's treachery is complete; he has usurped both his half brother and his father. If he can find Gloucester in the company of Lear, Edmund can ensure that Cornwall will dismiss any final doubts he might have about Gloucester's treachery.

Act III, Scene 6

Overview

Gloucester, Lear, the Fool, and the disguised Kent and Edgar have found shelter in a farmhouse near Gloucester's castle. Gloucester leaves briefly to gather supplies at the castle, while Kent notes that Lear has completely lost his sanity.

Edgar continues to rant of demons, while Lear decides to put Goneril and Regan on trial. He appoints Edgar as the judge. Kent tries to convince Lear to rest, because he believes the king will regain his sanity if he simply sleeps. Edgar finds Lear's true insanity so heartbreaking that he tells the audience that he may not be able to keep up his own act.

As Kent convinces Lear to lie down, Gloucester returns with bad news. Lear's life is in jeopardy. Gloucester advises Kent to take Lear to Dover, where the King of France awaits. Kent fears that waking Lear will mean that he will never recover, but letting him sleep will cost him his life. As Kent and the Fool carry Lear away,

Edgar realizes that his problems seem small compared with Lear's and decides to end his charade.

Analysis

The plot is moving quickly now—too quickly, in fact, for Lear, whose only hope lies in rest. Having driven Lear mad, Goneril and Regan now wish him dead. Cordelia's prediction is unfolding: Lear's life will only be safe with the youngest of his daughters, whose love is proved through action rather than through words.

Act III, Scene 7

Overview

Back at Gloucester's castle, Cornwall, Regan, Goneril, and Edmund are discussing the letter Gloucester received. Cornwall tells Goneril to inform Albany that the army of France has landed. Cornwall declares Gloucester a traitor, Regan says that Gloucester should be hanged, and Goneril suggests that Gloucester's eyes be plucked out. Cornwall sends Edmund off with Goneril, telling him that he will not want to see what Cornwall intends to do to Gloucester.

Oswald arrives with the news that Lear is on his way to Dover. As Goneril, Edmund, and Oswald leave, Cornwall orders servants to find Gloucester. Cornwall admits that he does not have the authority to order Gloucester's death, but he will punish him nonetheless.

The servants return with Gloucester, who reminds Cornwall that he is a guest in Gloucester's castle. Bound to a chair, Gloucester is questioned by both Cornwall and Regan about the letter he received from France. Gloucester

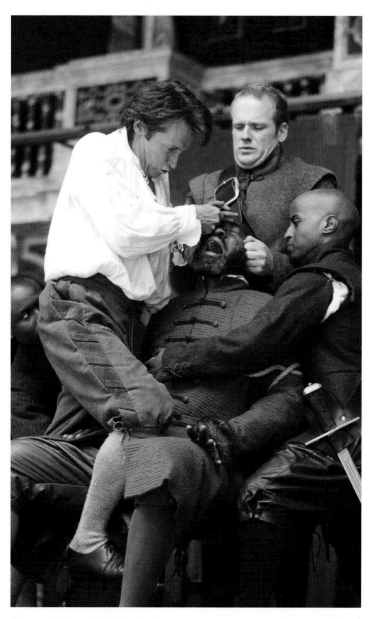

Gloucester (Joseph Mydell) is declared a traitor and loses his eyes as punishment.

claims that the letter was sent by a neutral party, one not opposed to Cornwall, but he admits that he sent Lear to Dover to protect him from Goneril and Regan, who were crueler to their father than they would have been to wolves.

Gloucester tells Regan that he will see revenge visited upon her and Goneril, but Cornwall replies that he will see no such thing and destroys one of Gloucester's eyes. When one of Cornwall's servants begs him not to take the other eye, Cornwall draws his sword. As the two men fight, Regan takes a sword from a second servant and stabs the first one from behind, killing him. Cornwall, himself wounded, then destroys Gloucester's other eye.

When Gloucester calls out for Edmund to avenge him, Regan reveals Edmund's treachery. Recognizing his mistake, Gloucester calls on the gods to protect Edgar. At Regan's order, Gloucester is thrown outside the gates of his own castle. Regan leads the wounded Cornwall offstage. Two of Cornwall's servants, horrified at the actions of their master and his wife, decide to deliver Gloucester to Edgar.

Analysis

The cruelty of Goneril and Regan toward Lear is matched by that of Edmund toward Gloucester. Edmund has not only usurped Gloucester, but also allowed Cornwall to take Gloucester's eyesight. Cornwall will pay the price for his own cruelty with his life. Gloucester's condition now parallels Lear's. Gloucester is not insane, but he is blind, and his blindness will lead him to desperation.

Act IV, Scene 1

Overview

On the heath, Edgar has returned to hope, having seen that Lear is worse off than he. Yet at that very moment, Gloucester arrives, led by an Old Man. The Old Man wants to stay with him, but Gloucester insists that he leave. Gloucester replies that he is better off now that he is blind than he was when he was prosperous and had the use of his eyes, when he stumbled, suspecting Edgar unjustly.

Edgar greets Gloucester and the Old Man. Gloucester again sends the Old Man away, though he asks him to bring Edgar some clothes. Gloucester asks Edgar if he knows the way to Dover. Edgar replies that he does and then speaks of demons, as he had the night before.

Gloucester gives Edgar his purse, which contains all the money that he has left. Gloucester asks Edgar to take him to a cliff in Dover, where he intends to jump into the sea.

Analysis

Lear's and Gloucester's stories continue to intertwine. While Edmund's actions toward Gloucester parallel those of Goneril and Regan toward Lear, Edgar's feelings toward his father are similar to Cordelia's feelings toward hers. Both Gloucester and Lear are headed to Dover, where their loyal children will rescue them.

Act IV, Scene 2

Overview

Goneril and Edmund have arrived at Albany's palace. Oswald, who has gone on ahead, greets them with the news that Albany seems to welcome the King of France's attack on Britain. Moreover, Albany has seen through Edmund's plot. To protect Edmund, Goneril sends him back to Cornwall, telling him that she hopes she can dispose of Albany and take Edmund as her husband.

As Edmund rides off, Albany arrives. When he last appeared, Albany had doubts about Goneril's treatment of Lear; now he believes that his wife's unfaithfulness to her father might forecast unfaithfulness to her husband as well. Goneril's actions toward Lear, Albany predicts, will lead to ruin, through the vengeance of either heaven or man.

Goneril accuses Albany of being a coward. Villains such as Lear and Gloucester, she says, deserve their punishment, even if it has been delivered before they have done anything wrong. Goneril tells Albany that he should be raising his troops against the King of France rather than complaining about her actions.

A messenger arrives with the news that Cornwall has died from his wound and reveals that the duke had put out Gloucester's eyes. Albany sees Cornwall's death as divine vengeance for Cornwall's treatment of Gloucester. The messenger gives Goneril a letter from Regan. Goneril fears that Regan might now pursue Edmund as her husband, but Goneril also sees this as an opportunity, because Edmund will now fill Cornwall's role.

Goneril leaves to answer Regan's letter, and Albany asks the messenger where Edmund had been when Cornwall

was putting out Gloucester's eyes. The messenger reveals that Edmund had plotted against Gloucester and then had left his father at Cornwall's mercy. Albany recognizes Gloucester's service to Lear and vows to avenge the loss of his eyes.

Analysis

Both Kent and Gloucester had suggested that Lear preferred Albany to Cornwall, and Albany now shows his loyalty to Lear. His loyalty rises above his marriage to Lear's daughter; in fact, Albany is loyal to the point of despising Goneril.

Act IV, Scene 3

Overview

Kent and Lear have arrived at Dover. Kent has left the king in the town and has gone to speak to the Gentleman with whom Kent had sent the letter for Cordelia. The Gentleman tells Kent that the King of France has had to return to his homeland but has left behind Cordelia and the Marshal of France to command his troops.

To Kent's questioning, the Gentleman replies that Cordelia had been moved to grief when she read Kent's letter. Kent sees in the Gentleman's description the proof of Cordelia's love. Kent declares that the stars must govern the lives of men, because there can be no other explanation for how different Cordelia is from Goneril and Regan. Lear, Kent says, occasionally recovers his wits, but refuses to see Cordelia—not because he is still angry with her, but because he is now ashamed of how he had treated the one daughter who truly loves him.

Analysis

Kent's remark about the stars governing the lives of men stands in contrast to Edmund's claim in Act I, Scene 2, that he would be the same man no matter which stars he was born under. Lear's shame over his treatment of Cordelia parallels Gloucester's recognition that he had wronged Edgar by suspecting him of disloyalty.

Act IV, Scene 4

Overview

In the French camp, Cordelia speaks with a doctor. Someone has seen Lear crowned with weeds and singing madly. Cordelia orders that her father be found and brought to her. The doctor holds out hope, though: all Lear needs is rest.

A messenger arrives with the news that British troops are descending on the French camp. The French, Cordelia says, are prepared.

Analysis

Kent had suggested that Lear might recover his senses if he rested, and the doctor echoes this. Nature can restore order if given the chance. Neither Cordelia nor Albany desires the battle that is coming. Both will fight it, however, for the same reason: out of loyalty to Lear, and in his defense.

Act IV, Scene 5

Overview

Back at Gloucester's castle, Oswald tells Regan that Albany is leading his army toward the French camp, though he

Lear (Derek Jacobi) wears a crown of weeds, which contrasts with both the crown he wore at the beginning of the play and his bare head.

seems reluctant to do so. Goneril, Oswald says, "is the better soldier."

Oswald has a letter from Goneril to Edmund, and Regan suspects that it has to do with Goneril's lack of love for Albany and her increasing affection for Edmund. But Regan tells Oswald that she has talked to Edmund, and the two of them are considering marriage now that Cornwall is dead. This, Regan suggests, may be good for Oswald, who has always been close to Goneril.

Regan gives Oswald a note to take to Edmund, instructing the steward to kill Gloucester if he should meet him on the way. Oswald would be happy to do so, he says, to prove his loyalty.

Analysis

Goneril and Regan, until now united against their father, are turning against each other. Both see in Edmund a kindred spirit, and Edmund's apparent willingness to kill his own father indicates that they are right.

Act IV, Scene 6

Overview

Gloucester and Edgar have arrived at Dover, where Gloucester intends to end his life by jumping off a cliff. Edgar is now dressed as a peasant in the clothes that the Old Man brought him.

Edgar tells Gloucester that they have arrived at the edge of the cliff and describes the scene below. Edgar can look no longer, he tells Gloucester, for fear of losing his own balance and falling. Gloucester is convinced and

Gloucester (Sergei Kuryshev) grapples with his suicidal tendencies, but Edgar (Daniil Kozlovsky) intends to save Gloucester's life.

asks Edgar to place him at the very edge. He gives Edgar a purse with a valuable jewel in it, then sends him away. In an aside, Edgar gives the audience the first indication that things are not what they seem; he is playing a trick on Gloucester, he says, in order to cure his despair. Gloucester prays and then throws himself forward, fainting as he falls.

The trick is revealed: Edgar and Gloucester are not on a cliff. Edgar approaches his father, pretending to be a man who, standing at the bottom of the cliff, watched him fall.

Edgar tells Gloucester that he has been saved by a miracle. Gloucester vows to bear his afflictions until the natural end of his life.

Lear enters, crowned with weeds as Cordelia had described. Though alone, Lear gives orders as if he were still the king at court. Gloucester says that he knows Lear's voice, and Lear, seeing Gloucester, compares him with Goneril. In his insanity, Lear sees clearly now that his daughters and the members of his court had flattered him for years. Yet Lear's two elder daughters and the courtiers had not meant any of it.

Edgar (Artem Osipov), Kent (Timofei Tribuntsev), Lear (Konstantin Raikin), and Gloucester (Denis Sukhanov) in a Russian production of *King Lear*.

Gloucester says that he knows the voice is that of the king, and Lear replies by pardoning an imaginary subject for the crime of adultery—the very crime that Gloucester had committed. Gloucester asks to kiss Lear's hand, but Lear says that his hand smells of death. When Gloucester asks Lear if he knows him, the king makes cruel jokes about Gloucester's eyes. But then Lear tells Gloucester that it is possible to understand the world without seeing it. Lear recognizes Gloucester and urges Gloucester to be patient—he will have revenge upon Albany and Cornwall (who Lear does not realize is dead).

The Gentleman that Cordelia sent to find Lear arrives with some attendants, and he orders them to grab hold of Lear. The king thinks that he is being taken prisoner, but the Gentleman tries to reassure him. When Lear declares that he is a king, the Gentleman tells him that he and the attendants obey Lear. That, Lear says, means there is hope. Lear then runs away, pursued by the attendants. The Gentleman tells Edgar that Albany's army will arrive within the hour. France's army has gone to meet Albany's, but Cordelia remains behind.

Gloucester asks the gods to take his life before he is tempted to commit suicide again. Edgar, still concealing his true identity, offers to lead his father to a place where he can stay. Just then, Oswald arrives and declares his intention to kill Gloucester. Gloucester is prepared to accept death, but Edgar intervenes. Adopting a strange accent, Edgar tells Oswald that if he does not leave Gloucester alone he will have to fight Edgar. Oswald attacks, and Edgar delivers him a mortal blow. Before he dies, however, Oswald begs Edgar to take the letters that he has been carrying and deliver them to Edmund, who is with Albany's army.

Reading the letter from Goneril to Edmund, Edgar discovers that she is urging his half brother to take advantage of the coming battle to kill Albany. If Edmund succeeds, Goneril will marry him; if he fails, she will have to remain married to Albany. Edgar plans to take the letter to Albany.

Gloucester laments that he is not mad like Lear, because then he would not suffer. As a drum heralds the arrival of the British army, Edgar leads Gloucester to safety.

Analysis

This scene, which marks the redemption of Gloucester, is built around a trick. The audience, watching Edgar lead his father to the edge of the "cliff," is as blind to what is about to happen as Gloucester is. Edgar gives a slight clue to his plan, but it is only after Gloucester has "fallen" from the "cliff" that the audience realizes that Edgar deceived his father in order to save his life. Like Kent with Lear, Edgar shows his loyalty to Gloucester through his actions.

The many references to demons Edgar made while in the guise of Tom o' Bedlam allow him to carry off his ruse. Since Gloucester believes in the gods and fate, he can see his survival as a miracle.

Act IV, Scene 7

Overview

In a tent in the French camp, Cordelia thanks Kent for his service to Lear and tells him that he should drop his disguise. Kent, however, asks Cordelia to let him keep it up for a while longer, and Cordelia agrees. She prays to the gods that Lear's insanity may be cured, and the doctor decides that it is time to wake him up. Lear is brought in,

Lear (John Bell) and Cordelia (Susan Prior) are reunited, and Cordelia again proves her unconditional love for her father.

carried in a chair. The doctor asks Cordelia to draw close to her father as they wake him. Cordelia kisses Lear and then reflects on the cruelties of her sisters.

As Lear awakes, Cordelia asks him how he is and whether he knows her. Lear is confused by his clothing and surroundings, and Cordelia thinks that he is still insane. However, as he comes to his senses, Lear replies that he thinks her to be his daughter Cordelia.

In sorrow, Lear tells Cordelia that he would drink poison if she wished. Cordelia cannot love him, Lear says, because of what he had done to her. She replies that she has no cause to hate him. The doctor declares that Lear is recovering but needs more rest. As Cordelia escorts her father from the tent, he begs her forgiveness.

The final battle is about to begin.

Analysis

As Kent had suspected, rest was all Lear needed to restore him to his true nature. As Lear comes to his senses, Cordelia asks him for his blessing, but he kneels before her instead. Cordelia tells him that he "must not kneel" because it is not fitting for a king to kneel even before his daughter. Lear's kneeling, however, is a sign that, in recovering his sanity, he has become better than he was before. Lear once enjoyed being flattered; now he wants to acknowledge his errors.

Act V, Scene 1

Overview

At the British camp, Edmund asks an officer to find out whether Albany intends to fight the French. Albany, Edmund says, has been changing his mind constantly; now it is time for him to make a final decision.

After the officer leaves, Regan once again declares her intention to marry Edmund, but she asks him whether his love for Goneril ever became physical. Edmund swears that it has not and never will.

As Albany and Goneril arrive, Goneril tells the audience that she would rather have Britain lose the battle than have Regan end up with Edmund. Albany explains the reason for his indecision: while the King of France is supporting Lear, the French are still an invading army.

Edgar enters, still in disguise, and asks to speak to Albany. As the rest leave to consult with the commanders of the British army, Edgar gives Albany the letter Goneril had written to Edmund, which Edgar had found on Oswald's body. Edgar urges Albany to read it before going into battle. He tells Albany that he will return when the duke has a herald blow a trumpet.

As Edgar leaves, Edmund enters. Edmund gives Albany an estimate of the size of the French army, which is now within sight. While Albany goes off to prepare, Edmund mulls over his situation. He has pledged his love to both Goneril and Regan, but he cannot have either "if both remain alive." Goneril will be angry if he marries Regan; but he cannot marry Goneril unless Albany is dead.

Edmund decides to accept Albany's help in the battle with the French, after which Goneril can devise some way to bring about her husband's death. Albany, Edmund fears, would show mercy to Lear and Cordelia, but with the duke dead, Edmund could protect his hard-won position by preventing their pardon.

Analysis

The division between Edmund and Edgar is reaching its climax, and it is mirrored in the increasing division between Goneril and Regan. Edmund cannot bear to leave anything to chance, and that will prove his downfall.

Act V, Scene 2

Overview

The battle has begun. On the field between the two camps, the army of France rushes forward, along with Cordelia and Lear. As all move out of sight, Edgar and Gloucester enter. Edgar tells his father to sit under a tree and pray for the success of the French forces. Edgar then follows the French army, only to return quickly. The battle has been lost; Lear and Cordelia have been taken prisoner. Edgar urges Gloucester to come with him, reminding Gloucester that he has vowed to let the gods determine his time of death. Gloucester leaves with his son.

Analysis

This short scene sets up the climax of the play and gives Gloucester one last chance to reaffirm his faith in the gods and fortune—a faith that is not mere fate, since the earl reaffirms it by agreeing to leave and thus save his life.

Act V, Scene 3

Overview

In the British camp, Edmund holds Lear and Cordelia prisoner. Cordelia asks whether she and Lear will see Goneril and Regan, and Lear replies that he would rather spend the rest of his days in prison in the company of Cordelia. Only death, Lear says, can part them.

Edmund orders Lear and Cordelia taken away and then calls a captain and hands him a note. Edmund has written instructions for how Lear and Cordelia are to be treated, and he promises to reward the officer if the instructions are carried out. He warns the captain that he cannot think about or question the instructions if he wishes to win Edmund's favor. The captain agrees and departs.

Albany, Goneril, and Regan arrive, and Albany praises Edmund's actions on the battlefield before asking Edmund to hand over Lear and Cordelia. Edmund gently refuses, saying that he has placed them under guard in order to prevent the British soldiers, who may still have sympathy

William Blake's depiction of Cordelia and Lear as Edmund's prisoners

for Lear and Cordelia, from turning against Edmund and Albany. Tomorrow, or sometime in the future, Edmund says, he will hand over Lear and Cordelia to Albany for trial.

Albany is angered by Edmund's answer, which seems to imply that Edmund regards himself not as Albany's subject but as his equal. Regan, however, intervenes: she intends to marry Edmund, thus making him Albany's equal; moreover, she says, Edmund's actions on her behalf have raised him to that status already.

Goneril objects that Edmund's actions are enough; he does not need Regan. As the sisters argue, Regan suddenly says that she does not feel well. She tells Edmund to take all of her possessions and her as well; she has taken him for her lord and master. Goneril once again objects, but Albany tells Goneril that granting permission for the marriage is not her right. Edmund replies that giving such permission is not Albany's right, either.

At that, Albany accuses Edmund of treason and Goneril of colluding with Edmund. Albany tells Regan that he cannot allow her to marry Edmund because Edmund is already spoken for: Goneril intends to marry him.

Albany calls for a herald to blow the trumpet. If no one comes forth to back his charge, Albany says, he will prove Edmund's treason through combat. Edmund maintains his innocence and pledges to fight Albany or any other who charges him with treason.

Regan again announces that she is sick, and Goneril indicates to the audience that she may have something to do with her sister's illness. Albany sends Regan to his tent as the herald arrives.

As the trumpet sounds a third time, Edgar arrives, still in disguise. He does not give his name but says that he is as noble as Edmund. Edgar orders Edmund to draw his sword to defend himself against the charges that Edgar now speaks: Edmund is a traitor to the gods, to Edgar, to Gloucester, and to Albany. Edgar dares Edmund to deny the charges, and when he does, the two half brothers fight. Edmund falls to the ground wounded, but Albany orders Edgar to spare Edmund's life. Goneril says that the combat proves nothing, because Edmund did not have to fight an opponent who refused to give his name.

Albany orders Goneril to be quiet and reveals her letter to Edmund. Goneril responds that the letter may be hers, but it does not matter; Albany cannot accuse her of treason, because she, not he, rules the kingdom. Goneril departs, and Albany sends an officer after her, saying that she is "desperate."

Edmund, near death, admits his treason and asks Edgar who he is. Edgar reveals his real name and says that Gloucester has suffered the loss of his eyes through divine justice because of his adultery, which brought Edmund into the world. Edmund now sees in his own downfall that same divine justice.

Edgar tells Albany and Edmund how he guided Gloucester and "saved him from despair." Just before the herald had sounded the trumpet, he had revealed the truth to Gloucester and asked his blessing in the coming combat with Edmund. Overcome with both joy and grief, Gloucester died. Edgar also reveals that Kent had disguised himself and served Lear as Edgar had served Gloucester.

A gentleman enters, holding a bloody knife. Goneril has killed herself after confessing to poisoning Regan, who has also died. Edmund says that he will join in death the two sisters to whom he had pledged marriage.

As Albany orders the bodies of Goneril and Regan to be brought out, Kent arrives, looking for Lear. Albany now remembers that he had come to demand that Edmund hand over Lear and Cordelia. Dying, Edmund tries to redeem himself by admitting that he had ordered the deaths of both Lear and Cordelia. Taking Edmund's sword as proof that his half brother has rescinded the order, Edgar runs to the castle to try to stop the captain. Before Edmund is carried away, he tells Albany that he and Goneril had ordered Cordelia to be hanged so that it would look as if she had committed suicide in despair.

Lear enters, carrying Cordelia and followed by Edgar and the captain. Lear calls for a mirror in the vain hope that Cordelia's breath will prove that she is still alive, though

Edgar is too late to stop Edmund's plot; Cordelia (Norah Krief) has been hanged.

he knows that she is dead. The sight is so horrifying that Kent asks whether this might be the end of time.

Abandoning hope, Lear announces that he killed the soldier who hanged Cordelia. Lear becomes aware of Kent, who admits that he has been serving Lear in disguise. Kent tells Lear that Goneril and Regan are dead. Albany believes that Lear has descended once again into madness.

A captain arrives to announce that Edmund is dead. Albany declares that he will return the throne to Lear and will restore Edgar and Kent to their rightful places.

His heart breaking as he mourns Cordelia, Lear dies. Kent urges that no one attempt to revive the king. Albany hands the rule of Britain over to Kent and Edgar, but Kent announces that he will soon join Lear in death. The play ends with Edgar becoming sole ruler of Britain.

Analysis

All of the threads come together in the play's final scene. Edmund, attempting to protect that which he has gained through deception, overreaches in presuming to place himself on the same level as Albany. Albany had intended to save Lear and Cordelia, but Edmund's treachery prevents it. As Albany had suspected, Goneril's disloyalty to Lear foreshadowed her disloyalty to Albany. Goneril's disloyalty extends even to Regan and to herself.

Until his battle with Edgar, Edmund continued to believe that he could make his own fate. Having been mortally wounded by his half brother's hand, Edmund finally realizes that Gloucester was right about the gods all along.

List of Major Characters

- Lear: King of Britain; father of Goneril, Regan, and Cordelia; and the protagonist of the play
- Goneril: First daughter of Lear and wife of the Duke of Albany
- Duke of Albany: Husband of Goneril; loyal to Lear in the end
- Regan: Second daughter of Lear and wife of the Duke of Cornwall
- Duke of Cornwall: Husband of Regan; puts out the Earl of Gloucester's eyes
- Cordelia: Third daughter of Lear and, later, queen of France; remains loyal to Lear despite being disowned by him
- Duke of Burgundy: Suitor to Cordelia; loses his interest in Cordelia after Lear disowns her

Tragedies As Comic Books?

RETELLINGS OF SHAKESPEARE'S stories aren't limited to typical novels. A new generation of writers and artists are putting their own spin on the Bard's classics, and they're thinking outside of the box. Recently, comic book artists and graphic novelists have begun adapting Shakespeare's work.

Ryan North is one such graphic novelist, who saw Shakespeare's potential for the genre. North thought that *Hamlet* would make a great choose-your-own-adventure book.

When North created a Kickstarter campaign in 2012 to fund his version of *Hamlet*, he hoped to raise $20,000. Yet North's idea proved far more popular than he'd hoped. His Kickstarter campaign reached its initial $20,000 goal in under four hours. Ultimately, 15,352 people gave a total of $580,905 to realize North's vision. At the time, this was the most money any Kickstarter campaign had ever raised. *To Be or Not to Be: That Is the Adventure* features illustrations from some of the biggest names in the world of comics. North's project has inspired its own adaptations. *To Be or Not to Be: That Is the Adventure* now has a board game, an audio book, and a play of its own.

KING LEAR (in 3 Panels)

King Lear is a jerk, and banishes his daughter.

Lear goes mad, wanders around a heath in a storm.

Almost everybody dies.

©2014 Mya Gosling

www.goodticklebrain.com

Mya Gosling's version of *King Lear* condenses the plot into a three-panel comic strip.

Ryan North isn't the only comic book artist getting into Shakespeare. Classical Comics is a publisher of graphic novels that has published illustrated versions of some of Shakespeare's most famous plays. Their adaptations are available in three formats. Readers can choose graphic novels featuring Shakespeare's original lines, lines "translated" into everyday English, or a quick summary of a play's dialogue.

Mya Gosling, creator of the web comic *Good Tickle Brain*, has an even more condensed approach to Shakespeare than Classical Comics does. While Gosling's web comic sometimes features stick figures recreating Shakespeare's plays scene by scene, it is most noted for comic strips summarizing entire plays in three panels.

Lear (Jonathan Pryce) with his three beloved daughters: Regan (Jenny Jules), Cordelia (Phoebe Fox), and Goneril (Zoe Waites).

- King of France: Suitor to Cordelia and, later, her husband
- Earl of Kent: Adviser to Lear; continues to advise Lear in disguise after the king banishes him from Britain
- Earl of Gloucester: Adviser to Lear and father of Edgar and Edmund; loses his eyes for remaining loyal to Lear
- Edgar: Legitimate son of Gloucester, half brother of Edmund, and, in the end, ruler of Britain; disguised as Tom o' Bedlam, guides Gloucester after the Duke of Cornwall puts out the earl's eyes
- Edmund: Illegitimate son of Gloucester and half brother of Edgar; attempts to usurp both his

brother and his father and pledges to marry both
Goneril and Regan

- The Fool: Lear's fool; remains loyal to Lear during
  the king's insanity and always tells him the truth,
  though often in riddle and rhyme
- Oswald: Steward to, and close confidant of, Goneril
- Doctor: A physician in the company of Cordelia;
  cures Lear of his insanity
- Old Man: one of Gloucester's tenants
- A captain: An officer under Edmund's command;
  sets Edmund's order to hang Cordelia into motion
- A herald: A messenger in the service of Albany;
  blows the trumpet that brings Edgar out of hiding
  to confront Edmund
- Various other Captains, Gentlemen, Attendants,
  and Servants

Analysis of Major Characters

Lear

In even more ways than may be obvious at first, King
Lear is the central character of the play. Lear's decision to
divide his kingdom sets the entire plot into motion. Lear
wishes to avoid strife in his kingdom after his death, but
his action brings strife into his kingdom while he is alive,
resulting in the deaths of all three of his daughters and
of Lear himself.

Lear's willingness to give up his kingdom reflects his
desire to forego his responsibilities. While he is upset when
Goneril and Regan demand that he reduce the number of

his knights, his daughters are right that the knights have grown riotous, reflecting Lear's own childlike behavior. The very contest that Lear devised to aid in dividing his kingdom—"Which of you shall we say doth love us most" (I.1)—is a child's game.

As the king of Britain, Lear personifies the kingdom. As he descends first into rage and then into madness, nature itself reflects the disorder in Lear's soul. The storm ends only when Lear realizes his errors, rests, and comes to his senses. Along the way, he gains a newfound humility, acquires the wisdom that the Fool told him he should have earned with age, and recovers his royal demeanor.

Cordelia

Of all of the characters in *King Lear*, only the Fool and Cordelia remain constant in their traits throughout the play. Yet while the Fool says that he always tells the truth to Lear, he admits that he lies to Goneril and Regan. Cordelia, however, never lies. When she refuses to take part in Lear's contest for the division of the kingdom, it is the depth of her love—not the lack of it—that compels her to remain silent. Cordelia cannot put that love into words because anything she says would be less than what she feels—in other words, it would be a lie. As Cordelia predicts to her sisters when she leaves with the King of France, she will prove through her actions that she loves Lear far more.

Lear's response is to disown Cordelia, and once the King of France has taken her for his wife, Cordelia could easily have lived the rest of her life with no duty to her father. Yet her love for Lear does not allow her to do so.

The King of France has spies in the households of both Goneril and Regan, and their reports of how Lear is being treated prompt Cordelia to come to her father's aid. France is the historical enemy of Britain, yet its forces invade to aid Cordelia's father—and thus to restore order to Britain, not to conquer it. Cordelia's death is a sacrifice of love, and through its senselessness, Shakespeare shows the depth and the constant nature of Cordelia's devotion to her father.

Gloucester

Gloucester is one of the most complex characters in *King Lear*. From the opening lines of the opening scene, we know that he has been unfaithful to his wife at least once, resulting in Edmund's birth. Gloucester's belated acknowledgment of Edmund, however, is a sort of faithfulness, an acceptance of the bonds of flesh and blood that would not have been required either in Lear's or in Shakespeare's time.

While Gloucester speaks of the role that the gods, nature, and fortune play in the lives of men, he does not blame his adultery on them. Gloucester takes responsibility for his actions.

Gloucester's loyalty puts him in an awkward position. His lands lie in the part of the kingdom that Lear gave to Regan and Cornwall, so Gloucester is naturally loyal to Cornwall; but his loyalty lies, above all, with Lear. Forced to choose, Gloucester chooses Lear, and that choice costs him his eyes and brings him to the brink of despair.

Gloucester's willingness to accept almost without question Edmund's claims against Edgar is itself a measure of the earl's faithfulness. Having acknowledged Edmund,

Gloucester does not doubt him; he assumes that Edmund has inherited his father's honesty.

Gloucester's misplaced loyalty brings him great regret, and his attempted suicide is motivated as much by his recognition that he has mistreated Edgar as by his desire to end his own misery. In his despair, Gloucester forgets his loyalty to the gods. Edgar's ruse does not so much restore his father's faith in the gods as it reminds Gloucester that his fate is not his own to decide. Relying now on the gods to determine when his life will end, Gloucester has restored his loyalty to nature, and to himself.

Edmund

If Gloucester is one of the most complex characters in the play, Edmund is the opposite. From the first moment he appears on stage alone, in Act I, Scene 2, Edmund is plotting and scheming against his half brother, Edgar. When he succeeds in usurping him, Edmund switches the object of his plot to Gloucester. With the earl out of the way after having been blinded and banished by Edmund's patron, Cornwall, Edmund sets his sights on both Cornwall's wife, Regan, and her sister Goneril.

The key to understanding Edmund is found in his three soliloquies in Act I, Scene 2. In the first, Edmund complains that others regard him as "base"—that is, ignoble—because of the circumstances of his birth and declares himself by nature better than Edgar.

In the second, Edmund mocks Gloucester's belief in signs and portents, saying that men who bring misfortunes on themselves are quick to blame "the sun, the moon, and the stars; as if we were villains on necessity." Edmund puts

Actor Vincent Guedon played Edmund in a 2007 production of *King Lear.*

no stock in such superstitions, yet he says, "I should have been that I am, had the maidenliest star in the firmament twinkled on my bastardizing." In other words, Edmund has chosen to live an immoral life and thus justifies those who call him "base." (I.2)

For Edmund, the only measure of right is success. Thus Edmund ends his third soliloquy with the line, "All with me's meet that I can fashion fit" (I.2)—that is, everything is right that I can make happen.

Edmund's villainy ends only as he lies dying, but even then his attempt to redeem himself is too little, too late: his actions have directly caused the death of Cordelia and indirectly the death of Lear.

Chapter Three

A Closer Look

Themes

Human Nature

In *King Lear*, characters often make reference to "nature" when they wish to present something as fixed or constant. The nature in question is not the natural world, but rather human nature or the proper ordering of human affairs, both within one's own life and with respect to others. "Nature" is not simply a way of saying what a person *is* but, even more importantly, of saying what a person *should be*.

Lear in particular speaks of his own nature and of the offenses offered against it by others. In Act I, Scene 1, Lear says that Kent's defense of Cordelia—especially his attempt to get Lear to break his vow to disown her—is one that neither "our nature nor our place can bear." Lear tells Kent that he has "never yet" broken a vow; it would be wrong not just for a man to do so, but even more so for a king. Lear's nature is more than the sum of his actions; it is both the source of his actions and the standard to which his actions must conform.

Because each person's nature is an objective standard, that nature must be respected by others. In other words, the natures of men must stand in their proper place with respect to one another. Lear's first error—his disavowal of Cordelia in Act I, Scene 1—came about, he says, when his most beloved daughter exhibited the "most small fault" of not making a show of her love for him. That action, "like an engine, wrench'd my frame of nature / From the fix'd place; drew from my heart all love / And added to the gall" (I.4).

Lear calls his own action a "folly" (I.4) that came about because he forgot his own nature. Later, when he leaves Goneril and expects to find sympathy from Regan, Regan tells him that "Nature in you stands on the very verge / Of her confine" (II.4). In other words, Lear, in the ravages of age, is finding it harder to act in accordance with his nature.

Lear's decision to divide his kingdom and divest himself of the authority that belonged to him by his nature has led to his mistreatment by others. Goneril and Regan owe Lear respect and loyalty on two accounts: because he is their king, and because he is their father (what Lear refers to in Act II, Scene 4, as "The offices of nature, bond of childhood, / Effects of courtesy, dues of gratitude"). When Lear gives up the exercise of his royal authority, however, he acts contrary to his nature, and Goneril and Regan no longer feel the need to respect his nature in any aspect—even as their father.

Cordelia, on the other hand, remains true to Lear in his true nature, even when he is mad—or, as Lear puts it, when "nature, being oppress'd, commands the mind / To suffer with the body" (II.4). By respecting his nature, both as father and as king, Cordelia is able to bring Lear back to his true nature.

In his final act—avenging Cordelia's murder—Lear, in accordance with his true nature, shows himself again both sovereign ruler and devoted father.

The Destructive Power of Rage

Closely related to the theme of the need to act according to one's nature is the theme of the destructive power of rage. All of the major characters in *King Lear*, with the notable exceptions of Cordelia, Edgar, and the Fool, fall into misfortune because they let their anger get the better of them. This is true even when the rage is, in some sense, justified, as in Lear's anger toward Regan, Goneril, and their husbands, and Kent's anger toward Oswald.

Lear's rage has drastic consequences. Lear banishes Cordelia from Britain and forces Kent to don a disguise, drives himself insane, and even upsets the order of the natural world, causing a tempest. At the height of his anger against Regan and Goneril—just before he departs from Gloucester's castle—Lear begs the heavens first for the "patience I need" to control his rage, and then for "noble anger." But Lear's rage overwhelms his nature as a father, and he swears "such revenges on you both" that "they shall be / The terrors of the earth!" His rage, he says, will keep him even from weeping for his daughters, which a father should do. Rage has altered his nature, and Lear declares to the Fool, "I shall go mad!" (II.4)

> *Lear.* I tax not you, you elements, with unkindness,
> I never gave you kingdom, call'd you children,
> You owe me no subscription.   *Act III. Scene II.*

Lear's rage is a destructive force that is mirrored by the tempest.

Immediately after Lear exits Gloucester's castle in Act II, Scene 4, a tempest begins, and when Gloucester returns, he confirms the cause: "The King is in high rage." When Kent goes looking for Lear and meets the Gentleman, the Gentleman speaks of the storm itself in a phrase that also describes Lear: "eyeless rage"—that is, blind rage (III.1). The storm will not subside—nor will Lear's sanity return—until Lear can rid himself of his rage through rest.

Cordelia recognizes this when, in Act IV, Scene 4, she sends the soldiers to find Lear as he wanders the countryside near Dover crowned with weeds: "Seek, seek for him, / Lest his ungoverned rage dissolve the life / That wants the means to lead it." "Ungoverned rage" stands in contrast to the "noble anger" for which Lear prayed, because the latter is placed in the service of wit or intelligence.

Against all of these, Cordelia stands in marked contrast. In Act IV, Scene 3, the messenger tells Kent that when he delivered the earl's letter to Cordelia, "It seemed she was a queen / Over her passion, who, most rebel-like, / Sought to be king over her." To which Kent replies, "O, then it moved her." and the messenger answers, "Not to a rage." Because she never lets rage overwhelm her nature, Cordelia is able to act properly to restore sanity to Lear and, thus, order to the natural world.

The Dangers of Moral Blindness

If the characters in *King Lear* often act against their nature and fall prey to rage, the chief reason is their moral blindness, as the stories of Lear and Gloucester show.

At the beginning of the play, Lear is old, but physically he can see well enough; he is incapable, however, of seeing the true nature of those around him. Lear thinks the words of flattery uttered by Goneril and Regan reflect true love, while Cordelia's unwillingness to commit her love to words means she is "untender" (I.1). In contrast, the King of France can see Cordelia's true nature, and he is willing to accept her as his wife despite Lear's unwillingness to provide her with a dowry.

Lear's moral blindness is reflected in his words. When Cordelia prepares to leave with the King of France in Act I, Scene 1, Lear mentions that he will never "see / That face of hers again." When Kent attempts to talk Lear out of his rash action toward Cordelia, Lear orders him, "Out of my sight!" Kent, understanding that the king's blindness is moral, replies, "See better, Lear, and let me still remain / The true blank of thine eye."

Lear's moral blindness toward Goneril and Regan lasts far longer than it should. Even after learning that Regan and Cornwall ordered the disguised Kent to be put in the stocks, Lear believes that Regan still loves him as she should. Faced with the evidence of his daughter's treachery, Lear turns back to Goneril, thinking that her ingratitude no longer looks as bad. When Lear finally recognizes that Goneril and Regan are morally the same, he loses control of himself and descends into madness.

Gloucester suffers from a similar moral blindness. Edgar has never given his father a reason to doubt him, yet Gloucester, out of affection for his newly acknowledged son, Edmund, falls prey to Edmund's plot.

Gloucester, Edmund says, is credulous—that is, too ready to believe that which he has been told, even if it contradicts his own experience. While Gloucester's loyalty to Lear helps him to come to his senses more quickly than Lear does, at least with respect to Goneril, Regan,

Blindness is a theme throughout the play. Many characters overlook important information, and Gloucester (Richard O'Callaghan) literally loses the ability to see.

and Cornwall, the damage has been done. Gloucester loses his eyes because he was blind to the true natures of Cornwall and Edmund (and Edgar, for that matter). After Regan orders the eyeless Gloucester cast out into the storm, Gloucester tells the Old Man who guides him, "I have no way, and therefore want no eyes; / I stumbled when I saw" (IV.1).

In other words, physical sight is less important than moral judgment. Lear, even in his madness, recognizes as much when he and Gloucester are reunited near Dover. Lear says to Gloucester, "Yet you see how this world goes" and when Gloucester replies that he sees "feelingly" (that is, with his hands, having no eyes), Lear replies: "What, art mad? A man may see how this world goes with no eyes" (IV.6).

The truly blind in *King Lear* are not those who cannot see, but those who cannot properly judge the true nature of others.

Motifs

Betrayal

Betrayal is one of the first motifs to emerge in *King Lear*, and also one of the most common. Throughout the play, each betrayal leads to another. In the opening lines, Gloucester reveals his betrayal of his wife, a betrayal that produced Edmund. Edmund, in turn, will betray Edgar and then Gloucester, and Edmund's plot leads Gloucester to disavow Edgar—another form of betrayal.

Lear views Cordelia's refusal to speak words of love as a betrayal and Kent's defense of Cordelia as the same. The Duke of Burgundy, when he finds out that Cordelia will not come with a dowry, drops any pretense at loving her—another betrayal.

Goneril and Regan, despite flattering Lear to gain their portions of his kingdom, betray him both as a father, through their insolence and ingratitude, and as their king, through their unwillingness to allow him to keep his knights, a symbol of what remains of his royal authority. Goneril betrays both her husband and Regan by pledging herself to Edmund. Regan betrays Goneril by asking Oswald not to deliver her sister's letter to Edmund, and Oswald, out of his own desire for Goneril, seems willing to betray Goneril by honoring Regan's request.

In the end, Edmund betrays more characters than any other, pledging marriage to both Goneril and Regan and betraying his allegiance to Albany by ordering Cordelia and Lear to be killed. Although he repents as he is dying, Edmund is unable to prevent the results of that betrayal—and thus betrays even himself.

Insanity

Insanity is the most obvious motif in *King Lear* because Lear spends all of Act III and most of Act IV in madness. Lear's rage overcomes his nature and physically weakens him, taking a toll on his mind. Having been flattered for decades by members of his court and by his two older daughters—who had disguised their true feelings—Lear is mentally unable to bear betrayal.

Insanity, however, is Lear's path back to reality. By taking leave of his senses, Lear allows his rage to flourish and wears himself out physically. He becomes more aware of the condition of those around him—not only of the fact that he has been lied to by those he most trusted, but also of the torments suffered by his subjects, such as Tom o' Bedlam, the insane beggar portrayed by Edgar.

Edgar's insanity is not real, but it has a similar effect. As Edmund noted in Act I, Scene 2, Edgar was "noble," with a nature that was honest and would not harm others. By pretending to be insane and thus experiencing the effects of insanity emotionally, he is able to guide Gloucester out of his despair and develops the character necessary to confront Edmund in the final scene.

Like Edgar, the Fool may seem to be insane to others, but his insanity is an act, a cover that allows him always to speak the truth to Lear. The Fool sees clearly from the beginning what Lear cannot see until he has lost his sanity and recovered it.

Lear (David Calder) must become insane to see the world as it truly is.

Symbols

Crown

The symbol of the crown does not appear very often in *King Lear*, but when it does, it is always significant. In Act I, Scene 1, before Lear himself enters for the first time, a coronet, or small crown, is brought into the palace. This crown is the symbol of Lear's royal authority, which he is about to give up. When Lear has divided his kingdom between Goneril and Regan and disavowed Cordelia, he orders Albany and Cornwall to divide the coronet itself between them as confirmation of the transfer of Lear's royal authority and property.

Immediately after Lear has done so, Kent rises to Cordelia's defense, saying that Lear is mad. Thus the crown is a symbol as well of Lear's wit or intelligence; the division of it is the first crack in Lear's sanity.

The crown next appears in Act I, Scene 4, when the Fool says to Lear, "Nuncle, give me an egg, and I'll give thee two crowns." The Fool plays on multiple meanings of *crown*. Lear, in dividing his royal authority, threw away the reason why others, including Goneril and Regan, respected him. The Fool talks of dividing the egg and eating the yolk—which represents Lear's wit—leaving Lear with two crowns (the white of the egg) with nothing in them. Driving the point home, the Fool contrasts "thy bald crown"—that is, Lear's head—with "thy golden one," his royal authority.

When Kent finds Lear wandering in the storm, he mentions the crown obliquely: "Alack, bareheaded?" (III.2). The lack of a crown symbolizes how far Lear has fallen and the loss of his wits.

At the height of his madness, Lear fashions a new crown out of weeds, which he is wearing when he encounters Gloucester near Dover. While still insane, Lear begins once again to act like a king, ordering members of the court around. The fake crown symbolizes the real authority, and the real wit, that Lear has by his nature. In wearing the crown of weeds, Lear prepares himself for the recovery of both his sanity and his authority.

Clothes

Just as the crown symbolizes more than Lear's royal authority, clothes in *King Lear* reflect deeper truths about the characters. When Lear objects to his daughters' plan to deprive him of his one hundred knights, he compares the knights to a woman's clothes. Clothes symbolize a man's authority and a woman's beauty. As Lear tells Regan, "Allow not nature more than nature needs"—that is, clothing that merely keeps one warm—and "Man's life is cheap as beast's" (II.4).

Edgar, in adopting the disguise of Tom o' Bedlam, removes all of the clothing that marked him as Gloucester's son and wraps his waist only in a blanket. The lack of clothing symbolizes the loss of sanity and intelligence. Seeing Edgar dressed that way, especially in a storm, Kent, Lear, and the Fool immediately think him mad.

Indeed, Lear, recognizing Edgar's madness, tears at his own clothes, symbolizing the loss of his own senses. Clothing, Lear says, separates the man from the beast, and Lear no longer desires to be a man.

When Edgar, still posing as Tom, is reunited with Gloucester in Act IV, Scene 1, the earl refers to Edgar

Lear tears at his clothes after his encounter with Tom o' Bedlam.

as "the naked fellow"—naked of both clothing and his senses. Gloucester asks the Old Man to bring Edgar some clothes. Once Edgar is dressed, Gloucester notes a change in Edgar's voice and manner of speech. Edgar denies it, saying, "In nothing am I changed / But in my garments." But the clothing reflects the changes that Edgar is going through. He is disguised now not to save himself but to try to bring Gloucester back from his despair.

Still, clothing can obscure reality, as Lear tells Gloucester when they are reunited near Dover: "Through tattered clothes small vices do appear; / Robes and furred gowns hide all" (IV.6). Clothes are a symbol of power; those who would flatter the powerful overlook their vices.

When Lear tore at his garments to become like Edgar, he shouted, "Come, unbutton here" (III.4). In the final scene, as he holds the dead Cordelia in his arms before dying himself, Lear asks for someone to "undo this button" and immediately slips back into madness, thinking that Cordelia is still breathing.

Language

Shakespeare's status as a master of the English language is unparalleled. Yet he had an advantage that most other writers have not: he made up the English language as he went along.

Shakespeare was writing at a time of enormous creativity in the English language. In *The Mother Tongue: English and How It Got That Way*, Bill Bryson notes that, from 1500 to 1650, "Between 10,000 and 12,000 words were coined, of which about half still exist." Shakespeare,

Showing the Sonnets Some Love

"Shall I compare thee to a summer's day?
Thou art more lovely and more temperate ..."

THESE LINES FROM Shakespeare's Sonnet XVIII have made their way into television shows and onto T-shirts. Yet most people think of Shakespeare firstly as a playwright, not a poet. The New York Shakespeare Exchange is working to bring more attention to the sonnets Shakespeare published in 1609—all 154 of them, in fact.

The theater company's artistic director, Ross Williams, wants to look beyond the legend of Shakespeare. He believes Shakespeare's words speak for themselves, so he created the Sonnet Project to let them shine. The project's goal is to "demystify Shakespeare's work and connect it to our own culture ... [to] really get into the heart of what Shakespeare can reveal to us, and about us." The Sonnet Project films actors performing Shakespeare's sonnets all around New York City, yet the actors don't merely recite lines. The team behind the Sonnet Project turns each sonnet into a mini-movie with cinematography that helps convey Shakespeare's meaning. Each location is selected to reflect this meaning, too. Viewers can select sonnets based on their number or based on the region of the city where they were filmed.

The project's scope is ever expanding. A big part of the project is finding ways to reach more people, so the New York Shakespeare Exchange created an iPhone/Android app in 2013. The app provides ready access to the sonnets that have already been filmed, as well as the new films as they are released.

The Sonnet Project is not the only outlet for videos of Shakespeare's sonnets, though. YouTube hosts almost forty thousand videos dedicated to Shakespeare's poems. On YouTube you can find videos explaining the cultural significance of his verse, famous actors reciting the sonnets, and lectures from universities around the world.

who lived for about fifty-two years in the middle of that period and whose writing was confined to less than three decades, contributed more than his fair share. According to Bryson, Shakespeare "used 17,677 words in his writings, of which at least one tenth had never been used before." (1)

In other words, Shakespeare may have coined almost one in every five new words between 1500 and 1650. When we look at individual years, Shakespeare's creativity seems even more astounding. In *A History of English Words*, Geoffrey Hughes examined the *Chronological English Dictionary* and found that "of the 349 new words and meanings recorded for 1605, the combined contributions of *Macbeth* and *King Lear* total 45 items or 12.8 percent."

Not all of those words entered into common usage. "Shakespeare," Bryson writes, "gave us the useful *gloomy*, but failed with *barky* and *brisky* (formed after the same pattern but somehow never catching on) and failed equally with *conflux*, *vastidity*, and *tortive*."

Hughes notes that Shakespeare was responsible for more than six hundred Latinate neologisms—new words formed from Latin roots. Thirty of those new words are found in *King Lear*, and at least five remain in common usage today.

Imagine being in the audience at the first production of *King Lear*. In one scene alone you would have heard Edmund deliver two of those neologisms. Complaining that others view him badly because he was conceived and born outside of wedlock, Edmund cries, "Why bastard? Wherefore base? / When my dimensions are as well compact, / My mind as generous, and my shape as true, / As honest madam's issue?" (I.2). *Generous* was a word unknown to Shakespeare's audience, and yet it is introduced here without any explanation. The same is true later in the

Shakespeare didn't just create plays and poems; he also created hundreds of new words.

King Charles II presided over the restoration in England, which began in 1660.

scene with *admirable*, when Edmund is mocking Gloucester for believing in fate: "An admirable evasion of whoremaster man, to lay his goatish disposition to the charge of a star!"

Other characters have an opportunity to make their mark on the English language as well. Verbally sparring with Oswald in Act II, Scene 2, Kent swears, "A plague upon your epileptic visage!" In Act IV, Scene 2, Albany, furious at Goneril for her treatment of Lear and fearing that she might be equally disloyal to him, declares, "Were't my fitness / To let these hands obey my blood, / They are apt enough to dislocate and tear / Thy flesh and bones." Thus *epileptic* and *dislocate* enter into the English language.

Not all of Shakespeare's neologisms are uttered by characters in the heat of passion. In Act IV, Scene 7, Cordelia awakens Lear with this fond wish: "O my dear father, restoration hang / Thy medicine on my lips, and let this kiss / Repair those violent harms that my two sisters / Have in thy reverence made!" A few decades after Shakespeare wrote *King Lear*, *restoration* would not only be in common use but would come to be the title of the age, after the monarchy was restored in England in 1660, following a little over a decade of rule by a Puritan Parliament. The restored king, Charles II, also brought about the restoration of public drama (including performances of Shakespeare's plays) after it had been outlawed for nearly two decades (from 1642–1660).

Interpreting the Play: Is *King Lear* One Play or Two?

Many of Shakespeare's plays exist in multiple versions, but the differences among the versions of King Lear have led some scholars to suggest that the two main versions should be treated as separate plays. Depending on which version of the text one consults, different themes are emphasized.

King Lear was first published in the First Quarto of 1608; a different version appears in the First Folio of 1623. The First Quarto contains about 285 lines not found in the First Folio, while the First Folio has between 100 and 130 lines (depending on how one counts a line) not contained

Eighty-two copies of the First Folio are part of the permanent collection at the Folger Shakespeare Library in Washington, DC.

in the First Quarto. That has led most recent scholars to conclude that the text of the First Quarto is drawn from Shakespeare's working papers, while the version in the First Folio represents the play as it was performed sometime before 1623. It is possible, though, that the version in the First Folio was edited before publication.

Complicating the matter is the fact that later editors created a hybrid version of the two texts, containing all the lines of both. That version is the one with which modern audiences are most familiar (and the one that is examined in this book). With recent scholarly editions of *King Lear* printing the quarto and folio versions alongside the hybrid form of the play, interpretations of Shakespeare's greatest tragedy are likely to become more varied rather than less so.

CHRONOLOGY

1564 William Shakespeare is born on April 23 in Stratford-upon-Avon, England

1578–1582 Span of Shakespeare's "Lost Years," covering the time between leaving school and marrying Anne Hathaway of Stratford

1582 At age eighteen, Shakespeare marries Anne Hathaway, age twenty-six, on November 28

1583 Susanna Shakespeare, William and Anne's first child, is born in May, six months after the wedding

1584 Birth of twins Hamnet and Judith Shakespeare

1585–1592 Shakespeare leaves his family in Stratford to become an actor and playwright in a London theater company

1587 Public beheading of Mary Queen of Scots

1593–1594 The Bubonic (Black) Plague closes theaters in London

1594–1596 As a leading playwright, Shakespeare creates some of his most popular works, including *A Midsummer Night's Dream* and *Romeo and Juliet*

1596 Hamnet Shakespeare dies in August at age eleven, possibly of plague

1596–1597 *The Merchant of Venice* and *Henry IV, Part One* are most likely written

1599 The Globe Theatre opens

1600 *Julius Caesar* is first performed at the Globe

1600–1601 *Hamlet* is believed to have been written

1601–1602 *Twelfth Night* is probably composed

1603 Queen Elizabeth dies; Scottish king James VI succeeds her and becomes England's James I

1604 Shakespeare pens *Othello*

1605 *Macbeth* is composed

1608–1610 London's theaters are forced to close when the plague returns and kills an estimated thirty-three thousand people

1611 *The Tempest* is written

1613 The Globe Theatre is destroyed by fire

1614 The reopening of the Globe

1616 Shakespeare dies on April 23

1623 Anne Hathaway, Shakespeare's widow, dies; a collection of Shakespeare's plays, known as the First Folio, is published

A SHAKESPEARE GLOSSARY

addition A name or title, such as knight, duke, duchess, king, etc.

affect To like or love; to be attracted to.

approve To prove or confirm.

attend To pay attention.

belike Probably.

beseech To beg or request.

bondman A slave.

bootless Futile; useless; in vain.

broil A battle.

charge Expense, responsibility; to command or accuse.

common A term describing the common people, below nobility.

condition Social rank; quality.

countenance Face; appearance; favor.

cousin A relative.

curious Careful; attentive to detail.

discourse To converse; conversation.

discover To reveal or uncover.

dispatch To speed or hurry; to send; to kill.

doubt To suspect.

entreat To beg or appeal.

envy To hate or resent; hatred; resentment.

ere Before.

eyne Eyes.

fain Gladly.

fare To eat; to prosper.

favor Face, privilege.

fellow A peer or equal.

filial Of a child toward its parent.

fine An end; "in fine" means in sum.

folio A book made up of individually printed sheets, each folded in half to make four pages. Shakespeare's folios contain all of his known plays in addition to other works.

fond Foolish.

fool A darling.

genius A good or evil spirit.

gentle Well-bred; not common.

gentleman One whose labor was done by servants. (Note: to call someone a *gentleman* was not a mere compliment on his manners; it meant that he was above the common people.)

gentles People of quality.

get To beget (a child).

go to "Go on"; "come off it."

go we Let us go.

haply Perhaps.

happily By chance; fortunately.

hard by Nearby.

heavy Sad or serious.

husbandry Thrift; economy.

instant Immediate.

kind One's nature; species.

knave A villain; a poor man.

lady A woman of high social rank. (Note: *lady* was not a
synonym for *woman* or *polite woman*; it was not a compliment
but simply a word referring to one's actual legal status in
society, like *gentleman*.)

leave Permission; "take my leave" means depart (with
permission).

lief, lieve "I had as lief" means I would just as soon;
I would rather.

like To please; "it likes me not" means it is disagreeable to me.

livery The uniform of a nobleman's servants; emblem.

Lord Chamberlain's Men The company of players
Shakespeare joined in London; under James I they became
the King's Men.

mark Notice; pay attention.

morrow Morning.

needs Necessarily.

nice Too fussy or fastidious.

owe To own.

passing Very.

peculiar Individual; exclusive.

privy Private; secret.

proper Handsome; one's very own ("his proper son").

protest To insist or declare.

quite Completely.

require Request.

several Different, various.

severally Separately.

sirrah A term used to address social inferiors.

sooth Truth.

state Condition; social rank.

still Always; persistently.

success Result(s).

surfeit Fullness.

touching Concerning; about; as for.

translate To transform.

unfold To disclose.

verse Writing that uses a regular metrical rhythm and is divided from other lines by a space.

villain A low or evil person; originally, a peasant.

voice A vote; consent; approval.

vouchsafe To confide or grant.

vulgar Common.

want To lack.

weeds Clothing.

what ho "Hello, there!"

wherefore Why.

wit Intelligence; sanity.

withal Moreover; nevertheless.

without Outside.

would Wish.

SUGGESTED ESSAY TOPICS

1. Compare Lear's relationship with his three daughters to Gloucester's relationship with his two sons.

2. Some scholars suggest that the Fool is really Cordelia in disguise. What evidence is there for this idea? What evidence is there against it?

3. What does Lear mean when he says, "I am a man / More sinned against than sinning"? Is he correct? Why or why not?

4. Once Edgar is no longer concerned about saving his own life, is his disguise really necessary? Why does he not reveal his true identity to Gloucester until the final scene of the play?

5. In the end, does fate or free will win out in the universe of King Lear? Support your answer with examples from the play.

TEST YOUR MEMORY

1. Why have Gloucester and Edmund been distant from each other in the past?
a) Edmund has been traveling abroad. b) Edmund lived with his mother rather than with Gloucester. c) Edmund was conceived out of wedlock. d) Edmund has been away at school.

2. Why does Burgundy not marry Cordelia?
a) Because Burgundy suddenly realizes that he does not love Cordelia. b) Because Lear will not give Cordelia a third of his kingdom. c) Because the King of France proposes to Cordelia first. d) Because Lear gives Cordelia the worst third of his kingdom.

3. In Act I, Scene 2, why does Edmund pretend he does not want to show the letter to Gloucester?
a) Edmund is trying to protect Edgar. b) Edmund does not want to upset Gloucester. c) Edmund is not sure whether Edgar wrote the letter. d) Edmund wants to make Gloucester more interested in the letter.

4. In Act II, Scene 1, why did Cornwall and Regan go to Gloucester's castle?
a) To seek Gloucester's advice concerning the dispute between Lear and Goneril. b) To hide from Lear and his knights. c) To help Gloucester in his search for Edgar. d) To seek shelter from the coming storm.

5. Why does Kent beat Oswald with the flat of his sword?
a) Because Oswald tells Kent to put his horse in the swamp.
b) Because Oswald refuses to draw his sword and fight Kent.
c) Because Kent wants Oswald to leave before delivering Goneril's letter to Regan. d) Because Kent suspects Oswald of being in love with Goneril.

6. Why does Lear insist that he be allowed to keep one hundred knights?
a) Lear needs the knights to help him on his hunts. b) The knights are a symbol of his former royal authority. c) Lear wants them for protection in case his daughters turn against him. d) Lear wants to reward the knights for their loyalty to him when he was king.

7. Why does the King of France decide to invade Britain?
a) Because his spies have told him of divisions between Albany and Cornwall. b) Because he is upset that Lear did not grant Cordelia a third of the kingdom. c) Because Kent has asked him to invade. d) Because Cordelia has tired of her husband and wants to return home.

8. Why does Lear attempt to tear off his own clothes?
a) Because they have been damaged by the storm. b) Because Lear wants to become a natural man, like Tom o' Bedlam.
c) Because Lear no longer wants any mark of his royalty. d) Because Lear wants to disguise himself for safety.

9. Why does Cornwall name Edmund the earl of Gloucester?
a) Because Gloucester has disappeared. b) Because Cornwall needs Edmund's support against Albany. c) Because Edmund reveals that Gloucester concealed a letter about the French invasion. d) Because Edmund bribes Cornwall to do so.

10. Why does Kent try to get Lear to sleep?
a) Kent is tired of listening to Lear's insane rantings. b) Kent knows that they cannot travel in the storm. c) Kent plans to betray Lear while he sleeps. d) Kent thinks that rest will help Lear recover his sanity.

11. Who first suggests that Gloucester's eyes should be plucked out?
a) Edmund b) Cornwall c) Regan d) Goneril

12. How does Cornwall die?
a) Regan stabs Cornwall after he puts out one of Gloucester's eyes. b) Edmund kills Cornwall for destroying Gloucester's eyes. c) Gloucester stabs Cornwall after he puts out one of Gloucester's eyes. d) One of Cornwall's servants mortally wounds him while defending Gloucester.

13. What convinces Gloucester that the gods saved him after he "jumped" from the cliff at Dover?
a) Edgar's claim that a demon had guided Gloucester to the edge of the cliff. b) Gloucester felt himself floating on the way down. c) Gloucester loses his sanity. d) Edgar reveals his true identity to Gloucester.

Answer Key

1. c; 2. b; 3. d; 4. a; 5. b; 6. b; 7. a; 8. b; 9. c; 10. d; 11. d; 12. d; 13. a

FURTHER
INFORMATION

Books

King Lear. Folger Shakespeare Library. Edited by Barbara A. Mowat and Paul Werstine. New York: Simon & Schuster, 2005.

King Lear. The New Cambridge Shakespeare. Edited by Jay L. Halio. New York: Cambridge University Press, 2005.

King Lear. The Oxford Shakespeare. Edited by Stanley Wells. New York: Oxford University Press, 2008.

Websites

Absolute Shakespeare
www.absoluteshakespeare.com

Absolute Shakespeare is a resource for the Bard's plays, sonnets, and poems and includes summaries, quotes, films, trivia, and more.

The Complete Text of Shakespeare's King Lear with Quarto and Folio Variations, Annotations, and Commentary
larryavisbrown.homestead.com/files/Lear/lear_home.htm

Compiled by Dr. Larry A. Brown, professor of theater at Lipscomb University in Nashville, Tennessee, this site offers an easy way to compare the various versions of the text of King Lear.

The Literature Network

www.online-literature.com/shakespeare/kinglear/

The Literature Network offers a straightforward presentation of the text of King Lear, with a very active forum discussing questions and issues raised by the play.

Play Shakespeare

www.playshakespeare.com

The Ultimate Free Shakespeare Resource features all the play texts with an online glossary, reviews, a discussion forum, and links to festivals worldwide.

William Shakespeare Info

www.william-shakespeare.info/site-map.htm

Extensive information on the life and world of Shakespeare, as well as texts of all the published works of Shakespeare, including King Lear.

Videos

Royal Shakespeare Company - King Lear, Act 4 Scene 2

www.youtube.com/watch?v=EUGeQd6J968

The Royal Shakespeare Company's staging of King Lear includes this argument scene between Goneril and Albany.

Sonnet 112

www.youtube.com/watch?v=a_M99aSNcT4

This video is the Sonnet Project's take on Shakespeare's Sonnet 112, filmed in Central Park.

BIBLIOGRAPHY

Bloom, Harold. *King Lear*. New York: Riverhead Trade, 2005.

Bloom, Harold, and Neil Heims, eds. *King Lear*. New York: Checkmark Books, 2008.

Bradley, A. C. *Shakespearean Tragedy: Lectures on Hamlet, Othello, King Lear and Macbeth*. New York: Palgrave Macmillan, 2007.

Bryson, Bill. *Shakespeare: The World as Stage*. New York: HarperCollins, 2007.

Elton, William R. *King Lear and the Gods*. Lexington: University of Kentucky Press, 1988.

Kahan, Jeffrey. *King Lear: New Critical Essays*. New York: Routledge, 2008.

Kahn, Paul W. *Law and Love: The Trials of King Lear*. New Haven, CT: Yale University Press, 2000.

Mack, Maynard. *King Lear in Our Time*. New York: Routledge (reprint edition), 2005.

Milward, Peter, S. J. *Shakespeare's Meta-Drama: Othello and King Lear*. Tokyo, Japan: Renaissance Institute/Sophia University, 2003.

North, Ryan. "To Be or Not to Be: That Is the Adventure." Kickstarter. Accessed May 12, 2015. https://www. kickstarter.com/projects/breadpig/to-be-or-not-to-be-that-is-the-adventure.

Pearce, Joseph. *The Quest for Shakespeare: The Bard of Avon and the Church of Rome*. San Francisco: Ignatius Press, 2008.

Rosenberg, Marvin. *The Masks of King Lear*. Newark: University of Delaware Press, 1992.

"The Sonnet Project." The Sonnet Project. Accessed May 12, 2015. http://www.sonnetprojectnyc.com.

Woodford, Donna. *Understanding King Lear: A Student Casebook to Issues, Sources, and Historical Documents*. Santa Barbara, CA: Greenwood Press, 2004.

INDEX

ABOUT THE AUTHOR

CAITLYN PALEY lives in Maryland, where she works in classrooms and writes books for students. In addition to writing the introduction for this book, Paley also wrote the introduction to *The Merchant of Venice* in the Reading Shakespeare Today series. She is the author of *Strategic Inventions of the Revolutionary War* and two books for middle school students (all from Cavendish Square). Paley enjoys doing research, hiking, and exploring the world. She hopes that her travels bring her to the Globe Theatre one day.